The Ultimate Guide to Launching Your Business

Step-by-Step Strategies for Beginners to Build and Scale Your occupation

Brandon T. Yu

All rights reserved. No part of this publication may be reproduced, distributed, or transmitted in any form or by any means, including photocopying, recording, or other electronic or mechanical methods, without the prior written permission of the publisher, except in the case of brief quotations embodied in critical reviews and certain other noncommercial uses permitted by copyright law.

Copyright © Brandon T. Yu, 2024

Chapter 1: Laying the Foundation: Defining Your Vision and Mission

- Importance of a clear vision and mission
- Crafting your business goals
- Aligning your personal values with your business purpose

Chapter 2: From Idea to Viable Business: Identifying Opportunities

- How to brainstorm business ideas

- Conducting market research
- Evaluating feasibility and scalability

Chapter 3: Building a Solid Plan: Crafting a Business Blueprint

- Key components of a business plan
- Financial planning and budgeting basics
- Setting realistic milestones and metrics

Chapter 4: Legal and Financial Setup: Getting Started Right

- Choosing the right business structure
- Registering your business and handling taxes

- Setting up business banking and funding options

Chapter 5: Marketing Made Simple: Reaching Your Audience

- Understanding your target audience
- Branding basics and creating a unique value proposition
- Effective low-cost marketing strategies

Chapter 6: Harnessing Technology: Tools and Platforms for Growth

- Essential tools for startups

- Building an online presence (website, social media, SEO)

- Leveraging automation and analytics for efficiency

Chapter 7: Navigating Challenges: Staying Resilient and Adaptable

- Common hurdles for new entrepreneurs

- Problem-solving and decision-making frameworks

- Building a support network and mentorship

Chapter 8: Scaling Your Business: Strategies for Sustainable Growth

- Identifying growth opportunities
- Hiring and building a team
- Adopting a mindset for long-term success

Chapter 1:

Laying the Foundation: Defining Your Vision and Mission

Every successful business begins with a strong foundation. Think of your business like a house. Before the walls go up, before the roof is secured, and before the paint dries, there must be a solid base to support everything. In the world of entrepreneurship, that foundation is your vision and mission. They are your guiding stars, the "why" behind everything you'll do, and the filter through which every decision will pass.

The Power of Vision

A vision is more than just a lofty dream; it's a vivid picture of the future you want to create. It's where you see your business heading in five, ten, or even twenty years. A strong vision captures your aspirations and provides clarity for not only you but also your team and stakeholders.

Take a moment to reflect on why you're starting this journey. What excites you about this venture? What problem are you solving, and how will the world be better because of your business? For example, if you're passionate about sustainable living, your vision might be to see a world where eco-friendly products are the norm, not the exception. A compelling vision inspires action and serves as a rallying cry during challenging times.

But a vision isn't just for dreaming—it's for doing. It's not enough to say, "I want to start a business." You need to define what success looks like. For instance, instead of saying, "I want to own a bakery," you could say, "I want to create a bakery known for the best gluten-free pastries in the city." Be bold in your vision. It should push you out of your comfort zone, yet remain achievable with determination and hard work.

Crafting Your Mission Statement

While your vision answers the question, "Where are we going?" your mission answers, "How will we get there?" It's the roadmap, outlining the steps you'll take to turn your vision into reality. A well-thought-out mission statement communicates your purpose, your core values, and the approach you'll take to achieve your goals.

Consider brands like Tesla, whose mission is "to accelerate the world's transition to sustainable energy." It's short, memorable, and leaves no doubt about what the company stands for. Your mission statement should do the same.

Start by identifying your target audience, the unique value you bring, and the problem you aim to solve. For example, if you're starting a fitness coaching business, your mission might be: "To empower individuals to achieve their health goals through personalized training, expert advice, and unwavering support."

A good mission statement is clear, concise, and actionable. Avoid jargon or overly complex language. Remember, this isn't just for you—it's for your customers, employees, and partners to understand why your business exists and how it operates.

Aligning Vision and Mission with Values

Your vision and mission become even more powerful when they are grounded in your personal and business values. Values are the principles that guide your behavior and decisions. They are the heart and soul of your business, shaping its culture and reputation.

Ask yourself: What matters most to you? Integrity? Innovation? Sustainability? Collaboration? When your vision and mission align with your values, you'll find it easier to attract like-minded customers, employees, and partners. Authenticity resonates, and people are drawn to businesses that stand for something meaningful.

Take, for instance, a startup that prioritizes diversity and inclusion. Their vision might be to create a world where opportunities are accessible to everyone, regardless of background. Their mission could focus on building platforms that connect underserved communities to resources and tools for success. These statements are powerful because they reflect not just what the business does, but what it believes.

Why This Matters More Than You Think

You might wonder: Why spend so much time on vision and mission? Can't I just start selling my product or service? The truth is, skipping this step is like driving without a destination. You might move fast, but you won't know where you're headed.

A clear vision and mission provide direction and focus. They help you prioritize tasks, allocate resources, and measure success. They also keep you grounded when things get tough—and they will get tough. When you're faced with difficult decisions, your vision and mission serve as a compass, reminding you of what truly matters.

Moreover, your vision and mission are your most powerful marketing tools. They differentiate you in a crowded marketplace, attract customers who share your values, and motivate employees to give their best. People don't just buy what you sell; they buy why you sell it.

Putting It All Together

Now that you understand the importance of defining your vision and mission, it's time to put pen to paper. Don't overthink it—this is a process, not a one-time task. Start with a rough draft and refine it as your business evolves.

Ask yourself:

What change do I want to see in the world?

How will my business contribute to that change?

What values will guide my actions and decisions?

Write your answers down, and use them as the basis for your vision and mission statements. Test them out. Share them with trusted friends, mentors, or potential customers, and see how they resonate.

Remember, a strong vision and mission aren't just statements—they're commitments. They represent the promise you're making to yourself, your customers, and the world. And when you have that clarity, you're not just starting smart—you're starting strong.

The Importance of a Clear Vision and Mission

Every successful journey begins with a destination in mind. Imagine setting out on a road trip without knowing where you're going—just driving aimlessly, hoping you'll end up somewhere worthwhile. The same goes for starting and running a business. A clear vision and mission are not just optional extras; they're the GPS and compass that guide you through the winding roads of entrepreneurship. They provide clarity, focus, and purpose, ensuring you stay on track no matter what challenges come your way.

Defining Vision and Mission

Before diving into their importance, let's clarify what these terms mean. A vision is your ultimate destination—the big picture of what you want your business to achieve. It's about imagining a future where your business has made a meaningful impact. A vision statement should inspire and challenge you, painting a vivid picture of the possibilities ahead.

On the other hand, a mission is the roadmap that gets you there. It explains the "how" of your business. It outlines the actions you'll take to bring your vision to life and serves as a daily reminder of why your business exists. While your vision is forward-looking, your mission focuses on the present, helping you stay grounded as you take practical steps toward your goals.

A Vision Gives You Purpose

One of the biggest reasons to have a clear vision is that it gives your business a sense of purpose. Without a purpose, it's easy to lose motivation or direction when the going gets tough—and trust me, it will. A strong vision keeps you grounded and reminds you why you started in the first place.

Consider some of the world's most iconic companies. Tesla's vision is "to create a sustainable future through clean energy," while Nike's is "to bring inspiration and innovation to every athlete in the world." These visions go beyond profits—they aim to make a difference. This higher purpose not only motivates the founders but also attracts like-minded employees, investors, and customers.

Your vision doesn't need to change the world on a global scale, but it should represent something meaningful to you. Maybe it's to provide affordable housing in your community, create unique handmade products that bring joy, or empower small businesses with innovative tools. Whatever it is, your vision becomes your North Star, ensuring every decision you make aligns with the impact you want to create.

A Mission Keeps You Focused

While your vision fuels your passion, your mission keeps you focused. It breaks your grand vision into actionable steps, making it easier to stay organized and on track. Without a mission, it's easy to get overwhelmed by all the possibilities or distracted by shiny new ideas that don't serve your ultimate goal.

A clear mission ensures you stay intentional about how you spend your time and resources. For example, if your mission is "to provide healthy, affordable meal options to busy families," every decision—from sourcing ingredients to pricing to marketing—should reflect that commitment. It helps you say "yes" to opportunities that align with your values and "no" to those that don't.

Building Trust and Credibility

In today's crowded marketplace, consumers aren't just looking for products or services—they're looking for meaning. People want to know that the businesses they support share their values. A clear vision and mission allow you to communicate your purpose effectively, building trust and credibility with your audience.

For example, Patagonia, a renowned outdoor clothing brand, has built a loyal following by staying true to its mission: "We're in business to save our home planet." This clear commitment resonates with environmentally conscious consumers who see their purchases as a way to support a cause they believe in.

When your vision and mission are authentic and well-defined, they become a powerful tool for differentiation. They make your business stand out and create a deeper emotional connection with your customers.

Attracting and Retaining Talent

A clear vision and mission don't just resonate with customers—they're equally important for attracting and retaining talent. Employees want to work for companies that have a sense of purpose. They want to feel like their efforts are contributing to something bigger than just the bottom line.

Imagine being part of a team where everyone is aligned around a shared vision and mission. It creates a sense of unity, drives collaboration, and fosters a culture of accountability. Employees who believe in your purpose are more likely to go the extra mile, show loyalty, and stay with your business for the long haul.

Guiding You Through Challenges

The entrepreneurial journey is filled with obstacles, uncertainties, and moments of doubt. During these times, a clear vision and mission act as your anchor. They remind you why you started and give you the courage to keep going, even when the odds seem stacked against you.

When faced with tough decisions, your vision and mission serve as a compass. Should you take on a lucrative project that doesn't align with your values? Should you pivot your business model? Should you expand into new markets? By staying true to your vision and mission, you can make decisions with confidence, knowing they're in line with your long-term goals.

How to Create a Clear Vision and Mission

If you don't already have a clear vision and mission, now is the time to create them. Start by asking yourself these questions:

What change do I want to see in the world?

How will my business contribute to that change?

What values are most important to me?

Once you have your answers, craft a vision statement that is bold, inspiring, and future-focused. Then, write a mission statement that is actionable, clear, and concise. Share these statements with your team, customers, and community, and use them as a daily guide for your business decisions.

Conclusion

A clear vision and mission are more than just statements—they're the heart and soul of your business. They give you purpose, keep you focused, build trust with your audience, and guide you through challenges. Whether you're just starting out or looking to refine your direction, investing time in defining your vision and mission is one of the smartest moves you can make. Remember, businesses that know where they're going are the ones that reach their destination—and beyond.

Crafting Your Business Goals

Imagine embarking on a journey without a map or destination in mind. You might stumble upon something worthwhile, but more often than not, you'll end up wandering aimlessly. The same holds true for running a business without clear goals. Goals are the backbone of your entrepreneurial journey, giving you direction, purpose, and a measurable way to track progress. Crafting well-defined business goals is not just a task to check off your list—it's a transformative process that turns your vision into actionable steps.

Why Business Goals Matter

At their core, business goals are your roadmap to success. They help you focus on what truly matters amidst the chaos of daily operations. Without goals, it's easy to get lost in endless to-do lists, chase shiny distractions, or burn out from lack of clarity.

Goals bring structure to your ambitions, breaking down your grand vision into manageable chunks. They answer the "what" and "how" questions: What are you trying to achieve? and How will you get there? With clear goals, you can allocate resources effectively, measure success, and pivot when necessary.

Moreover, goals foster accountability. Whether you're a solopreneur or leading a team, having clear objectives ensures that everyone stays aligned and committed. It's not just about working hard—it's about working smart, channeling energy into tasks that drive meaningful results.

Start with Your Vision

The process of crafting business goals starts with your vision. Think of your vision as the ultimate destination and your goals as the mile markers along the way. Before you can set goals, you need a clear understanding of where you want to go.

Ask yourself:

What do I want my business to look like in one year, five years, or ten years?

What impact do I want to create in my industry or community?

How will I know if I've succeeded?

Once you've answered these questions, you'll have a foundation to build your goals. For example, if your vision is to become a leading provider of sustainable clothing, your goals might include increasing market share, developing eco-friendly supply chains, or launching a new product line.

The Power of SMART Goals

Not all goals are created equal. Vague goals like "I want to grow my business" or "I want to make more money" are common pitfalls. They lack specificity, making it hard to track progress or stay motivated. That's where SMART goals come in—a tried-and-true framework to ensure your goals are clear and actionable.

SMART stands for:

Specific: Define exactly what you want to achieve. Instead of "I want more customers," say, "I want to acquire 500 new customers within six months."

Measurable: Quantify your goal so you can track progress. How will you know when you've achieved it?

Achievable: Be ambitious but realistic. Set goals that push you out of your comfort zone without setting yourself up for failure.

Relevant: Ensure your goals align with your vision and mission. Every goal should serve a purpose in your overall strategy.

Time-bound: Set a deadline to create urgency and accountability.

For example, instead of saying, "I want to increase sales," a SMART goal would be, "I want to increase monthly sales by 20% within the next three months by launching a targeted social media ad campaign."

Balancing Long-Term and Short-Term Goals

A common mistake entrepreneurs make is focusing solely on either long-term or short-term goals. Both are crucial, and finding the right balance is key.

Long-term goals are your big-picture objectives. They guide the direction of your business and require sustained effort over time. Examples include launching a new product line, expanding into international markets, or achieving a specific revenue milestone.

Short-term goals, on the other hand, are the stepping stones that help you reach your long-term aspirations. These might include completing a market research report, implementing a new customer relationship management (CRM) system, or training your team on new software.

By breaking your long-term goals into smaller, actionable short-term objectives, you create momentum and maintain motivation. Each small win brings you closer to the bigger picture.

Staying Flexible

While it's essential to set clear goals, it's equally important to remain flexible. The business landscape is constantly changing, and unforeseen challenges or opportunities may arise. A rigid adherence to your original goals can lead to missed opportunities or burnout.

Treat your goals as a living document—something you can adjust as needed. For instance, if you planned to expand to a new market but realized mid-way that your target audience requires more education about your product, it's okay to pivot. The key is to stay adaptable while keeping your vision in mind.

Tracking Progress and Celebrating Wins

Setting goals is only half the battle; tracking your progress is where the real magic happens. Regularly evaluate how you're doing and whether you're on track. This could involve weekly check-ins, monthly reviews, or quarterly strategy sessions. Use tools like spreadsheets, project management software, or goal-tracking apps to stay organized.

When you achieve a goal, celebrate! Acknowledging your wins—big or small—keeps morale high and reinforces positive behavior. It's a reminder that your hard work is paying off and motivates you to tackle the next challenge.

Common Pitfalls to Avoid

Crafting business goals isn't foolproof. Here are some common mistakes to watch out for:

Setting too many goals: Focus on a few key priorities rather than spreading yourself too thin.

Being vague: Ambiguity leads to confusion and inaction. Be as specific as possible.

Ignoring accountability: Share your goals with a mentor, partner, or team member to stay committed.

Failing to adapt: Don't be afraid to adjust your goals as circumstances change.

Conclusion

Crafting your business goals is a powerful process that bridges the gap between dreaming and doing. Clear, actionable goals not only give you direction but also keep you focused, motivated, and accountable. By aligning your goals with your vision, using the SMART framework, and balancing long-term aspirations with short-term actions, you'll set your business up for success. Remember, goals aren't just tasks—they're the steps that bring your vision to life. So grab a pen, start writing, and let your entrepreneurial journey begin!

Aligning Your Personal Values with Your Business Purpose

Building a business isn't just about making money—it's about creating something that aligns with who you are and what you stand for. When your personal values are in harmony with your business purpose, you create more than just a company—you build a legacy that reflects your beliefs and aspirations. This alignment not only strengthens your decision-making but also inspires trust and loyalty from your customers, team, and community.

The Power of Personal Values

Personal values are the core principles that guide your behavior and decisions. They're the beliefs you hold dear, the standards you live by, and the non-negotiables that shape how you interact with the world. These might include integrity, creativity, sustainability, empathy, or growth.

When these values are disconnected from your business purpose, you may find yourself feeling unfulfilled or out of sync with your work. On the other hand, when your business reflects your personal values, everything feels more authentic and meaningful. You're not just chasing profits—you're contributing to something bigger than yourself.

For instance, if one of your personal values is environmental sustainability, building a business that uses eco-friendly practices or promotes green products will feel naturally aligned. This connection keeps you motivated, even during tough times, because your work is tied to a cause you deeply care about.

Understanding Your Business Purpose

Your business purpose is the "why" behind what you do. It's more than selling products or providing services—it's the reason your business exists. A strong business purpose connects your company to a higher goal, offering value to your customers and contributing to the greater good.

Take time to reflect on why you're starting this business. Ask yourself:

What problem am I solving?

Who am I serving?

What impact do I want to create?

For example, a business purpose might be to make education more accessible, to empower underserved communities, or to bring joy to people's lives through art. When this purpose aligns with your personal values, your business becomes an extension of who you are.

Bridging the Gap: Aligning Values and Purpose

The real magic happens when you align your personal values with your business purpose. This process involves intentional reflection, planning, and action. Here's how to do it:

1. Identify Your Core Values
Start by listing your top five personal values. Think about what truly matters to you, both in your personal life and in the way you want to run your business. Are you passionate about fairness? Innovation? Family? Write these down and reflect on why they're important.

2. Define Your Business Purpose
Clarify the impact you want your business to make. This is where your values and purpose begin to intersect. For example, if you value community,

your business purpose might involve giving back through local partnerships or charitable initiatives.

3. Create Value-Driven Principles
Once you've identified your values and purpose, translate them into guiding principles for your business. These principles will inform everything from how you treat your customers to the way you market your products. For example:

If you value honesty, commit to transparent pricing and communication.

If you value creativity, emphasize innovation in your products or services.

If you value sustainability, adopt eco-friendly practices across your operations.

4. Incorporate Values into Daily Operations
Aligning values with purpose isn't a one-time exercise—it's an ongoing commitment. Look for ways to infuse your values into your daily business activities. For example:

Hiring employees who share your values.

Partnering with suppliers or organizations that align with your mission.

Using storytelling in your marketing to communicate your values to customers.

Why Alignment Matters

When your personal values align with your business purpose, the benefits are profound.

1. Authenticity and Trust
Customers are drawn to authenticity. When your business embodies your values, people can sense it. They'll trust your brand because it feels genuine and relatable.

For instance, a coffee shop that values community might host local events or donate a portion of profits to neighborhood initiatives. Customers will feel good about supporting a business that prioritizes connection over just profit.

2. Stronger Decision-Making
Every business owner faces tough decisions. When your values are clear, they act as a compass, guiding you through uncertainty. For example, if you value inclusivity, you might prioritize creating accessible products or services, even if it takes extra effort.

3. Employee Motivation and Retention
Employees want to work for companies that stand for something meaningful. When your business purpose aligns with clear values, it creates a sense of shared mission. This fosters loyalty, motivation, and a positive workplace culture.

4. Resilience in Tough Times
Entrepreneurship isn't always smooth sailing. There will be setbacks, failures, and moments of doubt. During these times, a values-driven business purpose provides clarity and motivation. It reminds you why you started and encourages you to keep going, even when things get hard.

Examples of Value-Driven Businesses

Let's look at a few examples of companies that successfully align values with purpose:

Patagonia: Known for its commitment to environmental sustainability, Patagonia's purpose is to save the planet. Its values are reflected in everything from its eco-friendly products to its activism campaigns.

TOMS: With a mission to improve lives through business, TOMS incorporates its value of giving back by donating a pair of shoes for every pair sold.

Ben & Jerry's: This ice cream company isn't just about delicious treats; it's also a champion for social justice, climate action, and community involvement.

These companies have built strong brands by staying true to their values and purpose, proving that profitability and principles can go hand in hand.

Staying True to Yourself

Aligning your personal values with your business purpose is a journey, not a one-time task. As your business evolves, revisit your values and purpose to ensure they remain aligned. Stay flexible, but never compromise on what matters most to you.

When your business reflects your values, it becomes a source of pride and fulfillment. It's not just a way to earn a living—it's a way to make a difference, leave a legacy, and stay true to yourself. So, take the time to align your values with your purpose. The result will be a business that feels authentic, resonates with others, and stands the test of time.

Chapter 2:

From Idea to Viable Business: Identifying Opportunities

Every great business starts with an idea—a spark of inspiration that excites you, intrigues you, and sets your imagination racing. But turning that idea into a viable business isn't just about enthusiasm; it's about identifying the right opportunities in the right market at the right time. The leap from idea to execution requires a mix of creativity, research, and strategic thinking. In this chapter, we'll explore how to turn your idea into a business that not only works but thrives.

The Genesis of a Business Idea

Most business ideas emerge from a simple observation: a problem that needs solving, a gap in the market, or an inefficiency in an existing system. Some of the world's most successful businesses started with someone asking, "What if there's a better way?"

For example, Airbnb was born when its founders realized people attending conferences struggled to find affordable lodging. Uber came to life because someone saw the inefficiency of traditional taxi services. These businesses didn't reinvent the wheel—they found a way to meet an existing need in a more innovative, convenient, or cost-effective manner.

The first step to identifying opportunities is to look around you. Observe your environment, listen to what people complain about, and consider the challenges you face in your own life. Ask yourself:

What frustrates me?

What do I wish existed?

What services or products could be improved?

Chances are, if you notice a problem, others have too. That's where opportunity lies.

Validating Your Idea

Not every idea is a good one. And even great ideas aren't always viable as businesses. This is why validation is critical—it's about testing your idea to see if it solves a real problem for real people who are willing to pay for a solution.

Start by defining your target audience. Who are the people most likely to benefit from your product or service? Get specific—age, income, location, lifestyle, and preferences. Once you've identified them, go out and talk to them. Conduct surveys, host focus groups, or even engage in casual conversations to gauge interest.

Ask potential customers questions like:

Does this idea solve a problem you face?

How much would you be willing to pay for a solution?

Are there existing products or services that address this need? If so, what's missing?

Validation doesn't have to be expensive or time-consuming. For example, if you're thinking about starting a food delivery service for busy parents, start by delivering meals to a few families in your neighborhood and collecting feedback. This hands-on approach gives you valuable insights while minimizing risk.

Researching the Market

Identifying opportunities also requires understanding the market. Who are your competitors? What are they doing well? Where are they falling short? By studying the landscape, you can find your unique value proposition—the thing that sets your business apart.

Start by analyzing your competitors. Look at their pricing, branding, customer reviews, and marketing strategies. Tools like Google Trends, social media analytics, and market research reports can provide valuable data on customer preferences and industry trends.

But don't just focus on what exists; think about what's emerging. Pay attention to new technologies, shifting consumer behaviors, and economic or cultural changes. For example, the rise of remote work created opportunities for businesses offering coworking spaces, virtual collaboration tools, and ergonomic home office products.

Refining Your Idea

Once you've validated your idea and researched the market, it's time to refine it. This involves narrowing your focus and creating a clear value proposition. A good value proposition answers three key questions:

1. What problem does your business solve?

2. How does your solution improve on existing options?

3. Why should customers choose you over competitors?

For instance, let's say your idea is a subscription box for pet owners. Your value proposition might be: "We deliver high-quality, eco-friendly pet toys and treats that are tailored to your pet's preferences—saving you time and helping the planet." This statement highlights the problem (finding sustainable pet products), the solution (customized subscription boxes), and the competitive edge (eco-friendliness and convenience).

Starting Small: The MVP Approach

Launching a business doesn't mean you have to perfect every detail from day one. In fact, one of the smartest strategies is to start with a Minimum Viable Product (MVP)—a simplified version of your product or service that solves the core problem without all the bells and whistles.

An MVP allows you to test your idea with real customers, gather feedback, and make improvements before investing significant time or money. For example, if your idea is a mobile app, start with a basic version that offers the most essential features. If it's a handmade jewelry line, launch with a small collection instead of a full catalog.

The beauty of an MVP is that it lets you learn and adapt quickly. If customers love your product, you can scale up. If they don't, you can tweak your approach or pivot to something else entirely.

Recognizing Opportunities Beyond the Obvious

Sometimes, the best opportunities are hidden in plain sight. Pay attention to niche markets or underserved communities. These are often overlooked by larger competitors but can be incredibly profitable for small businesses.

For example, while mainstream fitness brands focus on young, athletic audiences, a growing number of businesses are catering to seniors or individuals with disabilities. Similarly, niche food businesses like gluten-free bakeries or vegan meal kits have tapped into specific needs with great success.

The Role of Passion and Expertise

While market demand is crucial, don't overlook the importance of passion and expertise. Building a business takes time and effort, and your personal connection to the idea will help you stay motivated.

Ask yourself:

Am I genuinely excited about this idea?

Do I have the skills or knowledge to execute it?

If not, am I willing to learn or find the right partners?

When you combine passion with opportunity, you create a business that feels not only viable but also fulfilling.

Conclusion

Turning an idea into a viable business is a journey of discovery. It's about identifying real problems, validating your solutions, and finding your unique place in the market. With a combination of research, creativity, and adaptability, you can transform your spark of inspiration into a thriving business.

Remember, every successful entrepreneur started with an idea. What sets them apart is their ability to identify the right opportunities and take action. Now it's your turn to do the same. Keep your eyes open, your mind curious, and your ambition high—you never know where your next big opportunity might come from.

How to Brainstorm Business Ideas

Coming up with the right business idea can feel like a daunting task—especially when you're looking for something that will not only spark your interest but also meet a market need. Brainstorming business ideas, however, doesn't have to be an overwhelming experience. With the right mindset and approach, you can turn a blank page into a list of exciting possibilities. In this chapter, we'll explore how to tap into your creativity, explore various sources of inspiration, and refine those ideas into something truly viable.

Getting into the Right Mindset

Before you dive into the brainstorming process, it's important to set the stage mentally. You need to free yourself from self-doubt and limiting beliefs. The key is to remember that no idea is too small, too big, or too outlandish at first—everything is fair game in the brainstorming phase. The more open-minded you are, the more ideas you'll generate.

A great way to begin is to clear your mind. Find a quiet, relaxed space where you can think without distractions. Consider taking a few minutes to meditate or do some deep breathing exercises.

Relaxing helps to unlock your creative potential and lets your subconscious mind work its magic.

Start with What You Know

One of the easiest ways to come up with a business idea is to think about what you already know. Your experiences, skills, and interests are rich with opportunities for new businesses. Reflect on your background—have you worked in a particular industry, or do you have a hobby you're passionate about? Sometimes the most successful businesses arise from solving problems that you've encountered in your own life.

For example, if you've worked in the tech industry and noticed inefficiencies in project management tools, you might come up with the idea for a new app that addresses these gaps. If you're passionate about fitness and wellness, perhaps you could create a coaching service or a fitness product that fills a need you've identified. By tapping into your own expertise, you're more likely to come up with an idea that excites you and leverages your strengths.

Explore Market Gaps and Pain Points

Another effective way to brainstorm business ideas is to focus on identifying pain points and gaps in the market. These are problems that people face daily, yet solutions don't seem to be readily available—or if they are, they aren't meeting people's needs in a meaningful way.

Start by thinking about the products or services you currently use. Are there any frustrations or limitations you've experienced with them? If you've found yourself wishing for a better version of something, chances are, others feel the same way.

You can also conduct market research to identify gaps in the market. Browse online forums, social media groups, and review sites where people discuss products and services. Look for complaints, suggestions, or recurring themes. For example, if you notice that many people are dissatisfied with existing subscription box services, that's a potential opportunity to create a unique, niche subscription service that better meets the needs of your target audience.

Draw Inspiration from Trends

Trends are a great source of inspiration for new business ideas. Pay attention to emerging trends in technology, lifestyle, or consumer behavior. The key to capitalizing on trends is timing—finding an idea that's just beginning to take off before it becomes mainstream.

For instance, the rise of sustainable living and eco-conscious consumerism has given birth to countless businesses focused on eco-friendly products and services. Whether it's a zero-waste store, a reusable household product, or a sustainable fashion line, entrepreneurs are tapping into this growing movement.

Similarly, the explosion of remote work in recent years has opened up opportunities for businesses that serve the needs of digital nomads, home-office setups, and virtual collaboration tools. By keeping your finger on the pulse of current trends, you can spot ideas that have the potential to grow in the near future.

Engage in Creative Exercises

If you're feeling stuck or uninspired, don't worry—there are numerous creative exercises that can help spark new ideas. These activities encourage thinking outside the box and help you connect the dots between seemingly unrelated concepts.

A few effective exercises include:

Mind Mapping: Start with a central concept (e.g., "business ideas") and branch out into subtopics like "products," "services," "target audience," and "industry trends." Continue branching out until you've explored multiple angles.

Brainwriting: Similar to brainstorming, but instead of verbalizing ideas, you write them down. Set a timer for 5-10 minutes and write down as many ideas as you can without filtering or judging them.

Reverse Thinking: Take a common business model or product and think about how you could make it the opposite of what it currently is. What would a business look like if you flipped the problem on its head?

The goal of these exercises isn't necessarily to find the "perfect" idea right away but to generate as many possibilities as you can. Often, the best ideas emerge after you've jotted down dozens of initial thoughts, some of which can be combined or refined into something more focused.

Collaborate and Get Feedback

While brainstorming alone can be effective, collaborating with others can take your ideas to the next level. Share your thoughts with friends, family, or mentors who can offer fresh perspectives and constructive feedback. Sometimes, the right partner can help you refine an idea or point out aspects you hadn't considered.

If you're not sure whether your idea has potential, seek out feedback from your target market. You can conduct informal surveys, ask for opinions on social media, or even create a landing page to gauge interest. Understanding whether people are excited about your idea—or if it solves a real problem for them—is invaluable.

Think About Scalability and Feasibility

As you brainstorm ideas, it's important to consider the practicality of each one. Can the idea be turned into a business that can scale over time? Are there sufficient resources or markets available to support it?

Some ideas might be incredibly creative and exciting but not necessarily feasible from a business standpoint. On the other hand, ideas that seem straightforward at first can often be refined into scalable businesses if approached with the right strategy. Think about how you can scale your business idea: can it grow through technology, franchising, or digital marketing? How will you handle growth as demand increases?

Narrowing Down and Testing Ideas

Once you've generated a list of potential business ideas, the next step is to narrow them down. Evaluate each one based on factors like passion, market demand, competition, and feasibility. Which ideas excite you the most? Which ones feel the most aligned with your skills and experience?

Once you've chosen a few ideas to focus on, it's time to test them. This can involve developing a Minimum Viable Product (MVP), running a pilot program, or even just talking to potential customers. Testing allows you to refine your ideas and see how they perform in the real world before fully committing.

Conclusion

Brainstorming business ideas is a creative and exploratory process that combines inspiration, research, and practicality. The key to success lies in staying open-minded, exploring multiple angles, and refining ideas based on feedback and feasibility. Whether you draw inspiration from personal experiences, market gaps, trends, or creative exercises, the possibilities are endless. So, embrace the process, trust your instincts, and take the first step toward turning your ideas into a thriving business.

Conducting Market Research: A Guide to Understanding Your Market

Market research is one of the most crucial steps in turning your business idea into a successful venture. It provides the insights you need to make informed decisions about your products, services, target audience, and business strategy. Without proper market research, you're essentially sailing blind—you might have a great idea, but you won't know if people actually want it, how much they're willing to pay for it, or who your real competition is. In this chapter, we'll explore how to conduct effective market research that will give you a competitive edge and help you build a business that truly resonates with your customers.

Why Market Research Matters

Before we dive into the "how," let's take a moment to appreciate the "why." Why is market research so essential? The answer is simple: it reduces risk. Starting a business always comes with a degree of uncertainty, but market research helps you make better decisions by providing clarity on several fronts:

Understanding customer needs: You'll learn exactly what problems your target customers are facing and how your product or service can solve them.

Identifying market trends: You'll stay ahead of the curve by spotting emerging trends and adapting to changes in consumer behavior.

Analyzing competitors: You'll gain insights into what your competitors are doing well (and not so well) and learn how to differentiate your business.

Testing product ideas: You can gauge interest in your product or service before committing a significant amount of time and resources.

In short, market research helps you avoid costly mistakes, fine-tune your offerings, and develop a business model that is both sustainable and scalable.

Step 1: Define Your Research Goals

The first step in conducting market research is to define what you want to learn. Are you looking to understand customer preferences, gauge interest in a specific product, or analyze your competition? Setting clear goals will guide your research process and help you focus on gathering the right information.

For example, if you're launching a new mobile app, your research goal might be to understand what features potential users are looking for, or which existing apps are falling short. If you're starting a local restaurant, you might want to learn what dining experiences people are looking for in your area.

Having specific research goals in mind will help you decide on the type of data you need to collect and the methods you should use to gather it.

Step 2: Gather Primary Data

Primary data is information that you collect directly from your target audience. This data is fresh, specific to your business, and often more reliable than secondary data (which we'll discuss in a moment). The key to gathering useful primary data is to ask the right questions and use the right tools.

Here are a few methods you can use to collect primary data:

Surveys: Surveys are one of the most effective ways to gather quantitative data. You can use tools like Google Forms, SurveyMonkey, or Typeform to create online surveys that ask questions about customer preferences, demographics, and buying habits. Be sure to keep your surveys short and to the point to maximize response rates.

Interviews: One-on-one interviews give you a deeper, qualitative understanding of your customers' thoughts and feelings. You can conduct these interviews in person, over the phone, or via video calls. During these interviews, ask open-ended questions that encourage your customers to share their pain points, desires, and experiences.

Focus Groups: Focus groups are small, moderated discussions where you can gain insights into how people feel about your product or service. This method is particularly useful for testing new ideas, getting feedback on prototypes, or understanding consumer perceptions.

Observations: Sometimes, observing people in their natural environment can provide valuable insights. For example, you could visit local stores or cafes and observe how customers interact with products or services similar to yours.

Step 3: Collect Secondary Data

Secondary data is information that has already been collected by other sources. This type of data is usually easier and less expensive to obtain than primary data, but it's still incredibly useful. You can find secondary data in a variety of places, including:

Industry reports and studies: Many organizations publish free or paid reports on industry trends, market size, and consumer behavior. These reports can give you a broad understanding of your industry and highlight opportunities or threats you may have overlooked.

Government data: Government agencies often collect valuable demographic, economic, and market data. Websites like the U.S. Census Bureau or the Bureau of Labor Statistics provide data on population size, income levels, employment trends, and more.

Academic research: Universities and research institutions publish studies on various industries and markets. These can provide insights into consumer behavior, technological advancements, or economic shifts.

Competitor websites and reports: Analyze your competitors' websites, press releases, and other publicly available materials to gain a better understanding of their offerings, pricing strategies, and market positioning.

Secondary data is a great way to get a general sense of the market, industry trends, and consumer behavior, but it should be used alongside primary data for a more complete picture.

Step 4: Analyze Your Competition

No business exists in a vacuum, and your competition will play a key role in shaping your market research. To understand how you can stand out, you need to analyze your competitors' strengths and weaknesses.

Start by identifying your direct competitors—businesses that offer the same or similar products or services. You can also look at indirect competitors—businesses that offer alternatives or substitute products.

Once you've identified your competitors, gather information on:

Their products or services: What are they offering, and how does it compare to your idea?

Their pricing strategy: How much do they charge, and how does their pricing structure align with your target audience's willingness to pay?

Their marketing efforts: How do they promote their products or services? What platforms do they use?

Their customer feedback: Look at reviews and ratings on sites like Google, Yelp, or social media. What are customers saying about their experiences?

This competitive analysis will help you identify gaps in the market, understand consumer preferences, and spot opportunities to differentiate your business.

Step 5: Interpret Your Data

Once you've gathered your primary and secondary data, it's time to analyze it and draw conclusions. Start by organizing the data into categories, such as customer demographics, preferences, competitor analysis, and market trends.

Look for patterns, correlations, and insights that align with your research goals. For example, if you're conducting a survey to determine interest in your product, you might find that 70% of respondents express frustration with existing solutions—an opportunity to position your product as the ideal fix.

It's also important to validate your findings. Does the data support your business assumptions? Are there any unexpected insights that could change your approach? The goal is to use your research to make informed, strategic decisions for your business.

Step 6: Make Data-Driven Decisions

Finally, use the insights from your market research to guide your business decisions. Whether you're deciding on product features, refining your target market, or crafting your marketing strategy, data-driven decisions are more likely to lead to success.

For example, if your research shows a clear demand for eco-friendly products, you might choose to develop a sustainable product line. If you discover that your target audience values convenience, you could focus on providing a user-friendly customer experience.

Conclusion

Market research is an ongoing process that helps you understand your customers, competitors, and industry. By gathering and analyzing both primary and secondary data, you can make smarter decisions, reduce risks, and build a business that truly serves its target market. Whether you're just starting out or looking to grow, market research is the foundation of any successful business strategy. Keep researching, keep learning, and always be ready to adapt as your market evolves.

Evaluating Feasibility and Scalability: Turning Ideas Into Reality

When it comes to launching a business, having a great idea is just the beginning. To ensure that your idea doesn't remain just a dream, you need to evaluate its feasibility and scalability. These are two essential components of building a sustainable business. Feasibility helps you assess whether your idea can work in the real world, while scalability ensures that your business can grow and expand over time. In this chapter, we'll explore how to evaluate both the feasibility and scalability of your business idea, so you can confidently move forward with your entrepreneurial journey.

Understanding Feasibility

Feasibility refers to the practicality of your business idea. Is it something that can actually be done with the resources, time, and budget you have available? Is there a market demand for it? Will it solve a real problem or fulfill a need? A feasible business is one that can be launched, run, and sustained over time. Evaluating feasibility involves asking yourself some key questions that help you understand whether your idea can succeed in the real world.

1. Market Demand

First and foremost, you need to evaluate whether there is enough demand for your product or service. Even the most innovative ideas can fall flat if there is no market for them. This is where market research becomes invaluable. By talking to potential customers, analyzing trends, and assessing competitors, you can gauge the demand for your product. Ask yourself:

Does the product or service address a real problem or need?

Are people actively searching for solutions to this problem?

Is the target market large enough to sustain your business in the long term?

If you find that there is limited or no demand, it's better to pivot your idea before you invest too much time and money. On the other hand, if you discover a strong market demand, that's a positive indicator that your business idea is feasible.

2. Financial Feasibility

Money is often the make-or-break factor when it comes to starting a business. Financial feasibility involves estimating the costs involved in starting and running your business, as well as projecting potential revenue. You need to ask questions like:

How much money will it take to start the business (e.g., product development, marketing, equipment, legal fees)?

What are the ongoing operational costs (e.g., salaries, utilities, inventory, rent)?

How long will it take to break even or become profitable?

Developing a budget and creating a financial plan are essential to ensure that your business idea can be financially viable. If your projections show that your costs outweigh your revenue potential, you may need to reconsider your approach, refine your business model, or find ways to reduce expenses.

3. Technical Feasibility

If your business idea involves a product or service that requires technology or specialized skills, you need to assess whether you have the technical capabilities to bring your idea to life. For example, if you're developing an app, do you have the technical expertise to build it, or will you need to hire a developer? Or if you're launching a manufacturing business, do you have access to the necessary equipment and production processes?

In this stage, it's important to evaluate your own skills, the skills of your team, and whether external resources are required to execute your idea. Sometimes, a lack of technical knowledge can be overcome by bringing in the right people or partners.

4. Legal Feasibility

Every business needs to comply with legal requirements, and certain industries may have specific regulations or licenses you need to consider. Understanding the legal aspects of your business is crucial before you proceed. Consider the following:

What permits, licenses, or certifications are required to start your business?

Are there any intellectual property concerns, such as patents or trademarks?

What legal structure will you choose (e.g., sole proprietorship, LLC, corporation), and how will it impact taxes and liability?

Consulting with a lawyer or business advisor at this stage can help you navigate the legal landscape and avoid potential pitfalls.

Assessing Scalability

Scalability refers to your business's ability to grow without being hampered by limitations like its structure, resources, or market. A scalable business can expand smoothly, increasing revenue without a corresponding increase in operational costs. Scalability is crucial for long-term success and profitability. Let's break down how to evaluate whether your business idea is scalable.

1. Market Growth Potential

A scalable business needs a market that can support growth over time. When evaluating scalability, ask yourself if the market you're targeting will continue to grow or if it is a niche with limited potential.

Is your target market likely to expand in the future (e.g., through demographic trends, technological advancements, or changing consumer behaviors)?

Are there untapped markets or customer segments that you can explore?

For instance, if your business serves a rapidly growing sector, such as health tech or renewable energy, there may be significant room for growth. On the other hand, if you're targeting a market that is shrinking or already saturated, scaling your business might be more challenging.

2. Business Model and Operational Efficiency

A scalable business model is one that can handle increased demand without a proportional increase in costs. This means you need to have systems, processes, and resources in place that can be easily scaled as your business grows. Consider the following:

Can your product or service be produced at a larger scale without sacrificing quality?

Can you easily hire new employees or outsource tasks as needed?

Are your marketing and sales strategies effective at reaching a broader audience as your business expands?

For example, software companies often have highly scalable business models because their product (e.g., an app or platform) can be distributed to thousands or even millions of users with minimal additional costs. Similarly, online businesses can often scale quickly through digital marketing and automation tools.

3. Supply Chain and Infrastructure

As your business grows, you'll need to have a reliable and flexible supply chain in place. Scalability in this context means having suppliers, distributors, and infrastructure that can accommodate an increase in production or sales without disruptions.

Do your suppliers have the capacity to increase production if demand spikes?

Can you efficiently manage logistics, inventory, and fulfillment as orders increase?

Are your software and tech systems robust enough to handle larger volumes of data or transactions?

For instance, if you're running an e-commerce store and you plan to scale, your fulfillment process needs to be smooth, whether you're fulfilling orders yourself or working with a third-party logistics provider. The right technology and supply chain infrastructure will be key to ensuring scalability.

4. Financial Resources for Growth

Scalability often requires additional financial resources to expand. This could mean investing in new technology, hiring more staff, or increasing your marketing budget to reach a larger audience.

Do you have access to the capital needed to scale?

Can your business generate the cash flow required to fund expansion?

You may need to explore funding options such as loans, investors, or crowdfunding to fuel your growth. Having a clear financial plan for scaling is essential to avoid growing too quickly or running out of capital.

Conclusion

Evaluating the feasibility and scalability of your business idea is an essential step in turning it from a concept into a reality. By assessing market demand, financial feasibility, technical capabilities, and legal requirements, you can ensure that your idea is practical and viable. At the same time, evaluating scalability helps you plan for the long-term success of your business by considering market growth, operational efficiency, infrastructure, and financial resources. Both feasibility and scalability are about preparing for success, reducing risks, and laying the groundwork for a business that can thrive and expand in the future. With the right evaluation process, you'll be better positioned to make strategic decisions that lead to a prosperous and sustainable business.

Chapter 3:

Building a Solid Plan: Crafting a Business Blueprint

A business plan is the roadmap for your entrepreneurial journey. It serves as a comprehensive guide to help you navigate the challenges of starting and running a business, providing clarity on your objectives, strategies, and goals. Just like a blueprint is essential for constructing a building, a business plan is essential for constructing a successful enterprise. In this chapter, we'll explore the key components of a solid business plan and why it's crucial for your business's success.

The Importance of a Business Plan

At first glance, the idea of crafting a detailed business plan might seem daunting. You may wonder, "Do I really need a business plan?" The answer is a resounding yes. Whether you're seeking funding from investors, applying for a loan, or simply trying to clarify your own business vision, a well-structured plan is invaluable.

A business plan helps you:

Define your vision and mission: It clarifies what your business is all about and why it exists.

Identify your target audience: Understanding who you're selling to and what their needs are is key to building a successful business.

Set clear goals: A plan outlines your objectives and how you'll achieve them.

Anticipate challenges: It helps you foresee potential roadblocks and devise strategies to overcome them.

Attract investors or partners: A professional and well-thought-out business plan instills confidence in potential investors or partners.

A solid business plan provides the foundation for your business and serves as a guide to keep you focused and on track.

Key Elements of a Business Plan

A business plan is a detailed document, but it doesn't have to be overwhelming. Breaking it down into key components can make the process more manageable. Below are the essential sections that every business plan should include:

1. Executive Summary

The executive summary is the first section of your business plan, but it's often written last. It provides an overview of your entire plan, summarizing the key points, including your business concept, target market, and financial projections. Think of it as a pitch—a snapshot that grabs the reader's attention and entices them to read further.

The executive summary should include:

A brief description of your business: What problem does your business solve, and what makes it unique?

Your mission and vision statements: These should clearly communicate the purpose and long-term goals of your business.

Overview of products or services: What are you offering, and how will it benefit your target customers?

Financial summary: Briefly mention your financial projections, including expected revenue and profits.

Current business status: Are you just starting, or do you already have a product in the market?

Though the executive summary is concise, it plays a critical role in making a strong first impression.

2. Company Description

This section goes deeper into the specifics of your business. It should clearly define what your business is, what it offers, and the problem it solves. You'll also explain your business structure and the key players involved.

In your company description, include:

Your business name and structure: Will your business be a sole proprietorship, partnership, LLC, or corporation?

Business history: If your business is already established, provide a brief history. If it's a startup, explain the inspiration behind it.

Mission and values: Reinforce the guiding principles that will direct your business decisions.

Your team: Who are the key team members and what roles do they play in the company's success?

This section helps readers understand your business's foundation and how you intend to operate and grow.

3. Market Research

Market research is a critical component of your business plan. It demonstrates that you understand your industry, your competition, and your customers. This section will show that you've done your homework and that there's a viable market for your product or service.

In your market research section, include:

Industry analysis: What is the current state of the industry you're entering? Are there trends, growth opportunities, or challenges that you should be aware of?

Target market: Define your target audience, including demographic information like age, income, location, and lifestyle.

Competitive analysis: Identify your main competitors and evaluate their strengths and weaknesses. What makes your business different or better?

Market demand: Based on your research, how much demand is there for your product or service, and why will customers choose you over competitors?

This section provides the market intelligence that informs your business strategy and shows potential investors that there's an opportunity for growth.

4. Products or Services

In this section, you'll describe what you're offering in detail. Whether it's a product, service, or a combination of both, explain what makes it special and why it will succeed in the market.

Include the following details:

Product or service description: What exactly are you selling?

Unique selling proposition (USP): What makes your offering unique? Why should customers choose your product over others in the market?

Development and production: How will you produce your products or deliver your services? What resources are required, and how will you manage production?

Pricing strategy: How will you price your product or service? Will you offer any discounts, bundles, or incentives?

This section demonstrates that your product or service is well-thought-out and aligns with market needs.

5. Marketing and Sales Strategy

How will you attract customers and generate sales? The marketing and sales strategy outlines how you'll promote your business and convert leads into loyal customers.

In this section, you should include:

Branding and positioning: How will you position your brand in the market, and how will customers perceive it?

Marketing channels: What marketing methods will you use to reach your target audience (e.g., social media, email marketing, content marketing, influencer partnerships)?

Sales process: How will you handle sales? Will you have a physical store, an online shop, or a sales team?

Customer retention: What strategies will you use to retain customers and keep them coming back?

Your marketing and sales strategy should demonstrate a clear plan for customer acquisition and business growth.

6. Financial Projections

Financial projections are one of the most important sections of your business plan. Investors, lenders, and potential partners will want to see that you have a clear understanding of your financial needs and how you plan to generate revenue.

In this section, include:

Revenue projections: How much do you expect to earn in the first year, second year, and beyond?

Expense projections: What are your expected costs, including operating expenses, salaries, marketing, and production?

Profit and loss statement: A detailed forecast of your revenue and expenses to show when you'll reach profitability.

Cash flow analysis: How will money flow in and out of your business, and how will you ensure that you have enough to cover expenses?

Clear and realistic financial projections show that you're prepared to manage the financial aspects of your business and can be trusted with investments.

Conclusion

Crafting a business plan is more than just a formality—it's an essential step in turning your business idea into reality. A solid business plan provides structure and direction, helping you stay focused on your goals and make informed decisions. By thoroughly covering the executive summary, company description, market research, product offerings, marketing and sales strategy, and financial projections, you can create a roadmap for success. A well-written business plan will not only guide you through the startup process but will also demonstrate your commitment and preparedness to investors, partners, and stakeholders. So, take your time, put in the effort, and craft a business plan that truly reflects your vision for the future.

Key Components of a Business Plan: Building Your Blueprint for Success

When you embark on your entrepreneurial journey, having a clear and well-thought-out business plan is like having a detailed map for a road trip. It provides direction, helps you avoid potential pitfalls, and guides you toward your destination—success. A business plan is essential not just for securing funding or attracting investors, but also for clarifying your own vision and strategy. While the specifics of a business plan can vary depending on your industry and goals, there are key components that should always be included. These components ensure that your business plan is both comprehensive and effective. Let's dive into the crucial sections that every business plan should have.

1. Executive Summary: The First Impression

The executive summary is the opening section of your business plan, but it's often the last part you'll write. Why? Because it's a high-level summary of your entire business plan, capturing the essence of your vision, mission, market opportunity, and financial goals. It's your chance to grab the attention of potential investors, partners, or lenders.

In this section, you should provide a brief overview of:

Your business concept: What does your business do?

Mission and vision: What are your business's core purpose and long-term goals?

Product or service offering: What are you selling, and how will it benefit your target audience?

Market opportunity: Who is your target market, and why is your offering needed?

Financial projections: What are your revenue expectations, and when do you plan to break even or turn a profit?

The executive summary should be concise but compelling, offering just enough detail to entice the reader to continue.

2. Company Description: Introducing Your Business

The company description section provides a deeper look at your business and its structure. This is where you explain what your business is all about, why it exists, and the problem it aims to solve. Think of it as the "heart" of your business plan, as it lays the foundation for everything else.

Here's what should be covered in this section:

Business name and legal structure: Is your business a sole proprietorship, partnership, LLC, or corporation?

Industry background: What industry is your business a part of, and what trends or opportunities exist within it?

Your business's purpose: What problem are you solving, and why is your solution important?

Business goals: What are your short- and long-term objectives, and how will you achieve them?

Ownership and team: Who owns the business, and who are the key members of your team?

The company description should clearly articulate your business's mission, values, and the foundational reasons it exists.

3. Market Research: Understanding Your Industry and Audience

Market research is critical to the success of your business. It shows that you've done your homework and understand your market, customers, and competitors. A strong market research section demonstrates that there's a viable opportunity for your business, giving potential investors confidence in your ability to succeed.

In this section, include:

Industry analysis: What is the current state of the industry you're entering? Are there specific trends, challenges, or growth opportunities you should be aware of?

Target market: Who are your ideal customers? Include demographic details (age, income, education, etc.) and psychographics (lifestyle, values, interests).

Competitive analysis: Who are your competitors, and how do they compare to your business? What are their strengths and weaknesses, and how do you plan to differentiate your business?

Market demand: Based on your research, how large is your target market, and what is the demand for your product or service?

This section helps prove that there's a real market for your product and that you've identified where your business fits within the landscape.

4. Products or Services: What You're Offering

In this section, you'll describe your products or services in detail. It's important to explain how they solve your customers' problems or meet their needs. You should also highlight any unique features or advantages that set your offering apart from the competition.

For this part of the plan, include:

Product/service description: What exactly are you selling, and how does it work?

Value proposition: Why is your product or service valuable to customers? How does it solve their pain points or improve their lives?

Development stage: Are your products or services already in production, or are they still in the planning phase?

Pricing strategy: How do you plan to price your offerings, and why? Will you adopt a premium, competitive, or value-based pricing model?

Intellectual property: Do you have any patents, trademarks, or copyrights that protect your product or service?

This section should convey the benefits of your offerings and demonstrate how they stand out in the market.

5. Marketing and Sales Strategy: Reaching and Retaining Customers

No matter how great your product or service is, if people don't know about it, your business won't succeed. The marketing and sales strategy outlines how you plan to attract, convert, and retain customers. It explains how you'll make your target audience aware of your product and convince them to make a purchase.

Key elements to include:

Branding and positioning: How do you want your brand to be perceived in the market? What makes your brand unique, and how will it stand out?

Marketing channels: What methods will you use to promote your business (e.g., social media, content marketing, paid ads, partnerships)?

Sales funnel: What steps will potential customers take from discovering your product to making a purchase?

Customer retention: How will you ensure that customers return and become loyal advocates for your brand?

A well-thought-out marketing and sales strategy shows that you have a clear plan for growing your customer base and generating revenue.

6. Financial Projections: Mapping Your Financial Future

The financial projections section is one of the most crucial parts of your business plan, especially if you're seeking funding. It outlines your expected income, expenses, profits, and cash flow over a specific period—typically three to five years. Financial projections help you understand the financial health of your business and whether it has the potential to be profitable.

In this section, include:

Revenue projections: What are your sales expectations for each year? Include forecasts for both short-term and long-term growth.

Operating expenses: What are the ongoing costs to run your business (e.g., salaries, rent, utilities, marketing)?

Profit and loss statement: A detailed statement showing your income, expenses, and expected profits over time.

Break-even analysis: When do you expect your business to start turning a profit, and what are the key factors that will help you reach that point?

Cash flow projections: How will cash flow in and out of your business? Will you have enough cash on hand to cover expenses as you scale?

These financial details show that you're realistic about the numbers and prepared to manage the financial aspects of your business.

7. Appendices: Supporting Documents

Finally, the appendices section includes any additional supporting documents that strengthen your business plan. These may include:

Resumes of key team members

Market research data

Legal documents, contracts, or agreements

Product images or prototypes

Detailed financial statements

The appendices provide extra information that may be useful but isn't critical to the main body of the business plan.

Conclusion

A business plan is a vital tool for any entrepreneur. It helps you map out your business's goals, strategies, and financial outlook while also serving as a communication tool for investors and stakeholders. By including the key components—executive summary, company description, market research, products or services, marketing and sales strategy, financial projections, and appendices—you'll create a comprehensive and cohesive plan that can guide your business to success. Whether you're launching a startup or scaling an established business, your business plan will serve as a blueprint to navigate the exciting road ahead.

Financial Planning and Budgeting Basics: A Blueprint for Business Success

Financial planning and budgeting are the cornerstones of any successful business. Whether you're launching a startup or managing a growing enterprise, understanding how to manage your finances can be the difference between success and failure. Without proper financial planning, even the most innovative business ideas can fall apart due to mismanagement of resources or a lack of clear financial direction. In this chapter, we'll break down the basics of financial planning and budgeting, and how they work together to create a sustainable and profitable business.

The Importance of Financial Planning

Financial planning is the process of setting up a roadmap for how your business will allocate, manage, and grow its financial resources. It involves forecasting income, understanding expenses, estimating cash flow, and determining how to achieve your financial goals.

The key reasons financial planning is vital for your business include:

Direction and clarity: Financial planning provides a clear picture of where your money is coming from, where it's going, and how you can best utilize it to meet business objectives.

Mitigating risks: Through planning, you can anticipate potential financial challenges and create strategies to minimize risks.

Attracting investors: Investors are more likely to back a business that has a solid financial plan in place. It shows that you understand the financial mechanics of your business and are prepared for the future.

Sustaining growth: By forecasting financial needs and managing cash flow, financial planning enables you to scale your business without running into costly surprises.

The foundation of a successful business lies in how well you plan your finances. A good plan ensures you use your financial resources wisely and effectively to support both day-to-day operations and long-term goals.

What Is Budgeting, and Why Does It Matter?

Budgeting is a critical component of financial planning. A budget is essentially a plan for your income and expenses over a specific period, usually monthly or annually. It helps you allocate funds where they are needed most and ensures that you're not spending more than you earn. A budget is like a personal spending plan but on a larger scale, one that applies to your business.

The benefits of budgeting include:

Spending control: A budget helps you track where your money is going, ensuring that you don't overspend on unnecessary expenses.

Setting priorities: Budgeting allows you to allocate funds to the most critical areas of your business, such as product development, marketing, or customer service.

Forecasting and planning: With a clear budget, you can better forecast future revenues and expenses, ensuring that you are prepared for slow months or unexpected costs.

Cash flow management: A budget helps you monitor your cash flow, so you can ensure you have enough liquidity to cover bills, payroll, and other operational costs.

Without a well-managed budget, a business can quickly find itself in financial turmoil, unable to meet obligations or sustain its operations. Effective budgeting not only keeps your business afloat but helps it thrive, even in the face of fluctuating market conditions.

Key Steps in Financial Planning and Budgeting

Now that we've discussed the importance of financial planning and budgeting, let's walk through the key steps involved in creating a financial plan and budget that will guide your business to success.

1. Establish Clear Financial Goals

The first step in financial planning is setting clear, achievable financial goals for your business. These goals can be both short-term and long-term. Short-term goals might include covering startup costs, managing cash flow, or breaking even within the first year. Long-term goals could include reaching a specific revenue target, expanding into new markets, or building a substantial profit margin.

When setting goals, make sure they are SMART—Specific, Measurable, Achievable, Relevant, and Time-bound. For example, a SMART goal might be: "Increase monthly revenue by 20% over the next six months through an expanded marketing strategy."

2. Understand Your Income Sources

For any business, knowing where your income comes from is crucial. It's important to break down your revenue streams, whether they come from product sales, services, subscription models, or partnerships. By identifying and understanding these sources of income, you can better estimate future earnings and adjust your strategies accordingly.

If you have multiple income streams, track them individually to understand which sources are the most profitable and which may need improvement. This breakdown helps you prioritize areas for growth.

3. Track and Categorize Your Expenses

Just as income tracking is crucial, so too is understanding your business expenses. These expenses can be broken down into several categories:

Fixed costs: These are regular expenses that remain constant, like rent, utilities, salaries, and insurance premiums.

Variable costs: These fluctuate depending on production levels, such as raw materials, marketing expenses, or commissions for salespeople.

One-time costs: These are typically non-recurring expenses, like equipment purchases or legal fees.

Once you categorize your expenses, you'll have a clearer picture of where your money is going. This enables you to identify areas where you may be overspending or where you could cut back to improve your cash flow.

4. Build a Cash Flow Statement

A cash flow statement is a financial document that tracks the inflow and outflow of cash in your business. It's essential for understanding your liquidity—whether or not you have enough cash to cover day-to-day operations.

To build a cash flow statement, list all the expected sources of income (sales, investments, loans, etc.) and the expected expenses (rent, utilities, payroll, etc.). The goal is to ensure that you have enough cash coming in to meet your expenses and avoid running into a cash shortage. A positive cash flow means your business has more money coming in than going out, while a negative cash flow indicates the opposite.

5. Create and Monitor Your Budget

Once you've assessed your goals, income, and expenses, it's time to create your budget. A simple budget outlines your expected income and the amount you plan to allocate for each expense category over a specific period.

Your budget should be reviewed regularly (monthly or quarterly) to ensure that you are staying on track. Monitor how closely actual spending aligns with your budget and adjust as necessary. If you find that some costs are higher than expected, you may need to cut back in other areas or adjust your revenue goals.

6. Plan for Taxes and Savings

It's easy to overlook taxes and savings when you're focused on day-to-day operations, but both are vital for the long-term success of your business. Make sure to set aside a portion of your profits for taxes and establish a business savings fund to cover unexpected expenses or growth opportunities.

Consult a tax professional to ensure you're compliant with tax laws and taking advantage of any deductions or credits available to your business. Additionally, having a savings cushion will help you manage periods of low cash flow or fund important investments like equipment upgrades or marketing campaigns.

Conclusion

Financial planning and budgeting aren't just tasks to check off on a to-do list—they are vital processes that can make or break your business. A solid financial plan provides the roadmap for growth, while budgeting helps you stay disciplined and focused on your goals. By understanding your income, tracking your expenses, and managing cash flow, you can navigate the financial challenges of entrepreneurship with confidence.

The key is consistency—regularly revisiting and updating your financial plan and budget ensures that your business stays on course, adapts to changing circumstances, and thrives in the long run. So take the time to build a strong financial foundation, and watch your business grow and succeed.

Setting Realistic Milestones and Metrics: Your Roadmap to Business Success

When starting and growing a business, it's easy to get caught up in the excitement of new ideas, big plans, and lofty dreams. However, as much as vision and passion drive entrepreneurship, they need to be grounded in reality. That's where setting realistic milestones and metrics comes into play. These are not just arbitrary targets; they are carefully crafted checkpoints and measurements that guide your business toward sustainable success. They allow you to stay focused, measure progress, and adjust strategies when needed.

In this chapter, we'll explore the importance of setting milestones and metrics for your business, how to ensure they are realistic, and how they contribute to building a strong foundation for your company. By understanding and implementing the right milestones and metrics, you'll be able to navigate the complexities of entrepreneurship with confidence and clarity.

Why Milestones Matter

Milestones are critical because they break down your overarching business goals into smaller, manageable, and measurable steps. Instead of being overwhelmed by the idea of building a multi-million-dollar business, you can focus on achievable steps that lead to that larger vision.

The main reasons milestones matter include:

Progress tracking: Milestones act as markers that help you track progress toward your ultimate business goals. By setting clear checkpoints, you can step back, evaluate how far you've come, and assess whether your strategy is working.

Motivation and momentum: Every milestone you hit gives you something tangible to celebrate, which boosts morale and keeps the team motivated. It also helps prevent burnout by keeping the focus on incremental achievements rather than distant, daunting goals.

Course correction: Setting milestones allows you to assess whether your business is on the right track. If you're not hitting your targets, it's a signal that something may need to change, whether it's your marketing strategy, product offering, or operations.

Building credibility and trust: Reaching milestones can help build credibility with investors, partners, and customers. It demonstrates that you are making progress and meeting the commitments you've set for your business.

Think of milestones as the key steps in a journey; they provide direction and allow you to celebrate the small wins that accumulate into the larger picture of success.

The Importance of Realism in Setting Milestones

It's tempting to set big, bold goals right out of the gate. After all, who doesn't want to be the next big thing in their industry? However, setting unrealistic milestones can lead to disappointment, frustration, and financial strain. Unrealistic goals may also cause you to overlook the crucial daily tasks needed to keep the business running.

So, how can you set realistic milestones? The secret lies in assessing your current resources, capabilities, and market conditions. Here are some tips for making sure your milestones are achievable:

Start with what's possible: It's important to consider your current financial resources, team size, and business capacity when setting milestones. For example, if you're a solo entrepreneur, aiming for a hundred new customers in a month may be a stretch. Instead, set a goal of attracting ten customers in the next month and scaling gradually.

Break it down: While big goals are exciting, they can feel overwhelming. Instead of setting a single broad goal like "become profitable by year-end," break it down into smaller, achievable steps like "reduce monthly expenses by 10%" or "increase sales by 15% each quarter."

Account for external factors: The market, your competitors, and even global trends can impact your business's success. Consider these factors when setting milestones, as they'll help you understand what's realistic based on the current landscape.

Learn from experience: If you've been running your business for a while, use historical data as a guide. Review past performance, whether it's sales numbers, customer acquisition, or product development timelines. This will help you create more realistic projections based on actual results.

Remember, realistic milestones are not about underachieving or setting the bar low—they're about setting goals that are challenging but attainable, which helps keep your business grounded in the reality of what's possible.

Key Milestones to Set for Your Business

While every business is unique, there are a few key milestones that most entrepreneurs will need to achieve in their journey. These milestones can vary depending on your industry, market, and business type, but here are some examples:

Product Development: One of the first milestones for any business is getting your product or service to market. This includes completing product development, testing, and feedback loops, which leads to the launch of a final product or service.

Customer Acquisition: Building a customer base is essential for any business. Milestones around customer acquisition might include reaching a specific number of customers, generating your first sale, or achieving a targeted sales growth rate.

Profitability: For many businesses, achieving profitability is the ultimate milestone. This may come after securing your first steady stream of revenue, maintaining consistent growth, or reaching breakeven.

Market Expansion: Once you've successfully captured a market segment, the next milestone might be expanding into new geographical areas, industries, or customer segments.

Hiring Key Team Members: As your business grows, hiring the right team becomes a critical milestone. Building a strong team around you can help take your business to the next level.

Securing Funding: Whether through bootstrapping, angel investors, or venture capital, securing funding is an important milestone for many businesses.

Building Brand Recognition: Over time, your business will aim to become a trusted and recognized brand. Milestones here could include reaching a specific social media following, securing positive press, or being recognized within your industry.

Setting these types of milestones helps give you a clear roadmap of what needs to be accomplished and when.

How to Measure and Track Your Milestones

Once you've set your milestones, it's equally important to have a way to track and measure your progress. This is where metrics come into play. Metrics are quantifiable measurements that give you insight into how well you are achieving your milestones.

Some important metrics include:

Revenue growth: Tracking your revenue growth over time helps you see if your business is moving in the right direction.

Customer acquisition cost (CAC): This metric helps you determine how much it costs to acquire a customer, giving you insight into whether your marketing and sales efforts are efficient.

Conversion rates: Whether you're tracking website visits to sales, leads to customers, or email sign-ups to purchases, conversion rates are an essential metric for understanding your marketing effectiveness.

Customer retention: Keeping existing customers is often cheaper than acquiring new ones. Measuring customer retention rates helps you gauge customer satisfaction and loyalty.

Profit margin: Your profit margin gives you insight into how well your business is converting revenue into actual profit.

Once you establish these metrics, you can track them on a regular basis and make data-driven decisions to adjust your approach if needed.

Conclusion

Setting realistic milestones and tracking them with solid metrics is one of the most effective ways to steer your business toward success. Milestones break your big dreams into actionable steps, making the entrepreneurial journey more manageable and less daunting. By focusing on achievable goals and regularly measuring progress, you'll not only stay on track but also maintain the motivation and momentum needed to reach your ultimate business objectives.

Remember that your milestones should evolve with your business. As you grow, so too should the complexity and scope of your goals. Stay flexible, monitor your progress, and adjust your milestones as necessary to ensure that your business continues to thrive. With realistic milestones in place, your business is on the path to sustained success.

Chapter 4:

Legal and Financial Setup: Getting Started Right

Starting a business is an exhilarating journey filled with endless possibilities, but it's also a path that requires careful planning and attention to detail. One of the most crucial aspects of that planning is getting your legal and financial setup right from the beginning. These foundational steps will not only help you avoid costly mistakes but also give your business the protection, credibility, and structure it needs to thrive. Without a solid legal and financial foundation, your business may face unnecessary hurdles, from tax issues to potential lawsuits. In this chapter, we'll explore the critical steps in setting up the legal and financial sides of your business to ensure you're on the right track from day one.

Setting Up Your Legal Structure

The first decision you'll need to make when starting a business is choosing your legal structure. The legal structure of your business determines how it is taxed, how liabilities are handled, and the level of personal responsibility you'll have in case things go wrong. There are several options to consider, each with its own pros and cons:

Sole Proprietorship: The simplest and most common structure, a sole proprietorship means you are the sole owner and operator of your business. While it's easy to set up and manage, it also means that you are personally liable for any debts or legal issues that arise. This can be risky, especially if your business faces lawsuits or significant financial trouble.

Partnership: If you're starting a business with one or more partners, you may consider a partnership. A partnership allows multiple people to share ownership and responsibility for the business. However, just like a sole proprietorship, partners are personally liable for any business debts or legal problems unless you set up a limited partnership (LP) or limited liability partnership (LLP).

Limited Liability Company (LLC): An LLC combines the flexibility of a partnership with the liability protection of a corporation. LLC owners, known as members, aren't personally liable for the company's debts or lawsuits, which makes it a popular choice for small businesses. Additionally, LLCs offer more flexibility in terms of management and taxes.

Corporation (C-Corp or S-Corp): Corporations are separate legal entities from their owners, providing the highest level of protection for personal assets. However, they come with more complex regulations, including the need for a board of directors, bylaws, and regular filings. C-Corps are taxed separately from their owners, while S-Corps allow for pass-through taxation, meaning business profits are reported on the owners' personal tax returns.

Choosing the right legal structure is vital, as it affects everything from your personal liability to your tax obligations. Take the time to evaluate your options and consult a lawyer or accountant to ensure you make the best choice for your specific needs.

Registering Your Business

Once you've chosen your business structure, the next step is registering your business with the appropriate authorities. This usually involves filing the necessary paperwork with your local or state government, depending on your location and the nature of your business. Registering your business ensures that you are legally recognized as an official entity and can operate without the risk of legal complications.

Registering Your Business Name: If you're operating under a name other than your own, you'll need to register your business name, often referred to as a "doing business as" (DBA) name. This ensures that no other business can operate under the same name in your area.

EIN (Employer Identification Number): An EIN is like a social security number for your business. It is required for tax purposes, especially if you plan to hire employees or form an LLC or corporation. An EIN helps you open a business bank account, file taxes, and manage payroll.

State and Local Permits: Depending on your business type and location, you may need certain permits or licenses to operate legally. This can include health permits for restaurants, professional licenses for consultants, or sales tax permits for retailers. Be sure to research the specific requirements in your area to ensure compliance.

Opening a Business Bank Account

Once your business is legally established, it's time to open a business bank account. Keeping your personal and business finances separate is essential for both legal and financial reasons. A separate business account makes it easier to track expenses, handle taxes, and maintain accurate financial records.

When choosing a business bank account, consider factors like:

Fees: Some business accounts have monthly fees or transaction limits, so make sure you choose one that fits your budget and needs.

Features: Look for features like online banking, mobile deposits, and integration with accounting software to make managing your finances easier.

Customer Service: Good customer service is essential, especially if you encounter any issues with your account. Research the bank's reputation before committing.

Having a dedicated business account also helps protect your personal assets. If your business were to face legal trouble, having separate accounts ensures that your personal finances aren't tied up in the business's liabilities.

Understanding Business Taxes

One of the most crucial aspects of your financial setup is understanding your business's tax obligations. Regardless of your legal structure, your business will likely be subject to federal, state, and local taxes. Failure to comply with tax regulations can result in penalties, fines, or even the closure of your business.

Self-Employment Taxes: If you're a sole proprietor or a partner in a business, you'll need to pay self-employment taxes. This includes Social Security and Medicare taxes, which are typically withheld from employees' paychecks but are your responsibility as the business owner.

Income Taxes: Depending on your business structure, your business may be required to file an annual income tax return. LLCs and S-Corps generally pass profits through to the owner's personal tax returns, while C-Corps pay taxes separately.

Sales Tax: If you sell products or certain services, you may be required to collect sales tax from customers. This varies by state and local jurisdiction, so it's important to research the requirements in your area.

Payroll Taxes: If you have employees, you will need to withhold payroll taxes, including federal income tax, Social Security, and Medicare. You'll also need to pay unemployment insurance and other state or local taxes.

Consulting a tax professional early on is highly recommended to ensure you understand your obligations and set up your business in compliance with tax laws.

Managing Business Finances

Once your legal setup is in place, it's time to start managing your finances. Financial management is key to keeping your business running smoothly and ensuring its long-term success.

Budgeting: Creating a detailed budget is essential for managing cash flow, anticipating expenses, and identifying areas where you can save money.

Bookkeeping: Accurate bookkeeping is necessary for tracking income, expenses, and profits. You can choose to manage your books manually, use accounting software, or hire a bookkeeper to ensure your financial records are up to date.

Cash Flow Management: Maintaining a positive cash flow is essential for keeping your business operational. Monitor your accounts receivable and payable closely to ensure you have enough liquidity to cover operational costs.

Good financial practices, such as regularly reviewing financial statements and making strategic decisions based on your cash flow, will help your business stay financially healthy.

Conclusion

Getting your legal and financial setup right from the beginning is essential for building a strong foundation for your business. From choosing the right legal structure to understanding your tax obligations and managing your finances, these steps lay the groundwork for long-term success. While the paperwork and legalities may seem overwhelming at first, they are vital for protecting both your business and your personal assets. Taking the time to get things right now will save you from future headaches and ensure that your business is built on solid ground. By getting your legal and financial setup in order, you can focus on what matters most: growing your business and achieving your dreams.

Choosing the Right Business Structure: Laying the Groundwork for Success

Starting a business is an exciting and bold decision, but before diving into your entrepreneurial journey, one crucial step must be taken: choosing the right business structure. Your choice of structure will impact everything from your daily operations to how much you pay in taxes, and even your personal liability. It's not a decision to be made lightly, as the legal structure you select will shape the future of your business in profound ways. Whether you're a solo entrepreneur or planning to build a team, understanding the different types of business structures and selecting the one that best fits your vision is essential for long-term success.

In this chapter, we'll break down the various business structures available, their pros and cons, and the key factors you should consider to make an informed decision. By the end, you'll have a clear understanding of which structure aligns with your goals and how to move forward with confidence.

The Four Main Business Structures

When it comes to starting a business, there are four primary legal structures to consider: sole proprietorship, partnership, limited liability company (LLC), and corporation (either C-Corp or S-Corp). Each structure offers different levels of liability protection, tax treatment, and management flexibility, so it's important to assess which one is the best fit for your needs.

Sole Proprietorship

A sole proprietorship is the simplest and most common form of business structure. It's the default structure for a one-person business. In a sole proprietorship, you as the owner are the business. There is no legal distinction between the business and yourself, meaning all profits and losses are tied to your personal finances.

Pros:

Simplicity: Setting up a sole proprietorship is straightforward and requires minimal paperwork. There's no need to file special documents with the government to get started (though you may need to register a "doing business as" or DBA name).

Complete control: As the sole owner, you have complete control over every aspect of the business, from decision-making to day-to-day operations.

Tax simplicity: Income from a sole proprietorship is reported on your personal tax return, which simplifies the tax process and eliminates the need for separate corporate tax filings.

Cons:

Unlimited personal liability: The major downside of a sole proprietorship is the lack of liability protection. Since the business and personal finances are legally the same, you are personally responsible for any debts or legal actions against the business.

Limited growth potential: Because sole proprietorships tend to be small, they may face challenges in raising capital or expanding beyond a single owner/operator.

Partnership

If you're starting a business with one or more partners, a partnership may be the best structure. A partnership allows two or more individuals to share ownership and responsibilities for the business. Partnerships can either be general partnerships, where all partners share equally in both profits and liabilities, or limited partnerships, where one or more partners have limited liability.

Pros:

Shared responsibility: Partners can share the workload, bringing their expertise and skills to the table. This can make running the business easier and less stressful for each individual.

Tax advantages: Like a sole proprietorship, a partnership has pass-through taxation, meaning the business itself doesn't pay taxes. Instead, profits and losses are passed through to the partners' personal tax returns.

Flexibility in management: Partnerships allow for a high level of flexibility in structuring the business and how decisions are made, especially if you opt for a limited partnership with differing levels of involvement.

Cons:

Joint liability: In a general partnership, all partners are equally liable for business debts and legal issues. This can be risky, especially if one partner mismanages the business or if the business faces significant debt.

Potential for conflict: Disagreements between partners can occur, especially when it comes to decision-making, profit-sharing, or the direction of the business. It's essential to have a clear partnership agreement to avoid future conflicts.

Limited Liability Company (LLC)

A Limited Liability Company (LLC) is a hybrid business structure that combines the simplicity and flexibility of a partnership with the liability protection of a corporation. LLCs are ideal for entrepreneurs who want to protect their personal assets while maintaining control over the business.

Pros:

Liability protection: One of the biggest advantages of an LLC is that it shields your personal assets from business debts and legal actions. This means your home, car, and personal savings are safe from creditors if the business faces financial issues.

Flexibility in taxation: An LLC can choose how it wants to be taxed. By default, it's treated as a pass-through entity (like a sole proprietorship or partnership), but it can also elect to be taxed as an S-Corp or C-Corp if that's more advantageous.

Operational flexibility: LLCs have fewer formal requirements than corporations. You don't need a board of directors, and there's no need to hold annual meetings, making it easier to manage.

Cons:

Self-employment taxes: LLC members are typically considered self-employed and must pay self-employment taxes (Social Security and Medicare) on their share of the profits. However, this can be mitigated by electing S-Corp taxation if applicable.

State-level regulations: LLCs must adhere to state-specific regulations, which can vary widely. Some states impose annual fees or taxes on LLCs, which can add to the overall cost of maintaining the business structure.

Corporation (C-Corp and S-Corp)

Corporations are the most complex business structure, but they offer the greatest level of personal liability protection and can be an excellent option for businesses looking to scale or attract investors. There are two main types of corporations: C-Corporations (C-Corps) and S-Corporations (S-Corps).

C-Corp: A C-Corp is a separate legal entity from its owners, meaning it can enter into contracts, own property, and pay taxes independently of its shareholders. One of the main benefits of a C-Corp is the ability to issue multiple classes of stock, making it easier to raise capital from investors.

Pros:

Strong liability protection: As a separate legal entity, a C-Corp provides the highest level of liability protection for its owners. Shareholders are not personally liable for business debts or legal issues.

Ability to raise capital: C-Corps can issue shares of stock to attract investors or raise funds through venture capital.

Tax advantages: C-Corps can deduct business expenses, including employee benefits, which can result in tax savings.

Cons:

Double taxation: One of the biggest downsides of a C-Corp is double taxation. The corporation itself pays taxes on its profits, and then shareholders are taxed again when they receive dividends.

Complexity and cost: Operating a C-Corp requires more paperwork, formalities, and regulatory compliance than other business structures. This makes it more expensive to maintain.

S-Corp: An S-Corp is a special type of corporation that allows profits to pass through to shareholders' personal tax returns, thus avoiding double taxation.

Pros:

Pass-through taxation: Like LLCs, S-Corps avoid double taxation. Shareholders report the business's profits on their personal tax returns, reducing the overall tax burden.

Limited liability: S-Corp shareholders have the same personal liability protection as C-Corp owners.

Cons:

Ownership restrictions: S-Corps can have no more than 100 shareholders, and all shareholders must be U.S. citizens or residents.

Strict eligibility requirements: To qualify for S-Corp status, the business must meet several specific conditions, including being a domestic corporation and having only one class of stock.

Factors to Consider When Choosing a Business Structure

Choosing the right structure depends on several factors, including:

Liability protection: Do you want to shield your personal assets from business risks?

Taxation: Are you prepared to handle self-employment taxes, or do you want pass-through taxation?

Control: How much control do you want over the business?

Growth plans: Are you planning to expand and raise capital, or are you content with a smaller-scale operation?

Each structure offers different advantages, so it's important to evaluate your needs, business goals, and long-term plans when making a decision.

Conclusion

Selecting the right business structure is one of the most important decisions you'll make as an entrepreneur. Whether you opt for a sole proprietorship, partnership, LLC, or corporation, understanding the legal and financial implications will help set your business up for success. Take your time, do the necessary research, and consult with legal and financial experts to make the best choice for your unique situation. With the right structure in place, you'll be positioned to thrive in the competitive world of entrepreneurship.

Registering Your Business and Handling Taxes: The Essentials for Success

Starting a business is an exciting adventure, but it's also one that comes with a lot of responsibility.

Once you've got your business idea, goals, and structure sorted out, the next important step is registering your business and understanding the taxes you'll be responsible for. Both of these tasks lay the foundation for operating your business legally and avoiding any future headaches. While navigating registration and taxes may feel overwhelming at first, having a clear understanding of the process will help you stay organized, focused, and compliant with the law.

In this chapter, we'll break down the essential steps involved in registering your business and handling taxes so you can confidently move forward on your entrepreneurial journey.

Registering Your Business: Making It Official

The first step to operating your business legally is registering it with the appropriate authorities. This process may vary depending on where you live and the structure of your business, but there are some common steps every entrepreneur needs to follow.

1. Choosing and Registering Your Business Name

Your business name is a vital part of your brand identity. It's how potential customers will find and recognize you, so it's important to choose a name that resonates with your target audience and reflects your brand's values. However, before you get too attached to a name, you need to make sure it's available and legally usable.

To do this, conduct a business name search through your local or state government's business registration website. This will ensure that no one else is already using the name. If the name you want is taken, you'll have to choose another or tweak it to make it unique. In some cases, you may also need to register a DBA (Doing Business As) name, which is a legal way to operate your business under a name that's different from your legal business name.

2. Deciding on a Legal Structure

As we discussed earlier, choosing the right legal structure for your business is essential. Whether you opt for a sole proprietorship, partnership, LLC, or corporation, this decision affects your taxes, liabilities, and the way your business is organized. Once you've settled on your structure, the next step is filing the necessary paperwork with your state or local government to make your business officially registered.

For example, if you're forming an LLC, you'll need to file Articles of Organization with your state's Secretary of State office. Corporations require Articles of Incorporation. Sole proprietorships and partnerships may require less paperwork but still need to be registered, especially if you plan to operate under a name other than your own.

3. Applying for an Employer Identification Number (EIN)

An Employer Identification Number (EIN), also known as a Federal Tax Identification Number, is a unique number assigned to your business by the IRS. It functions like a Social Security number for your business and is required for tax purposes. You'll need an EIN if you plan to hire employees, open a business bank account, or if you're structured as an LLC or corporation.

You can easily apply for an EIN online through the IRS website, and the process is free. The EIN will be used for various legal and financial purposes, including tax filings, opening accounts, and tracking business transactions.

4. Registering for State and Local Licenses or Permits

Depending on your location and the type of business you plan to run, you may need to obtain specific state or local licenses or permits. For example, if you're opening a restaurant, you might need a health department permit. If you plan to sell goods, you may need a sales tax permit.

Each state and municipality has different requirements, so it's important to research what's required in your area. Failing to obtain the necessary licenses and permits can result in fines or legal complications, so don't skip this step.

Handling Taxes: A Crucial Part of Your Business Journey

Once your business is officially registered, the next step is understanding your tax responsibilities. Taxes are an inevitable part of business, and staying on top of them is crucial to your success. Whether you're running a small startup or a larger company, understanding your tax obligations will save you time, money, and stress in the long run.

1. Understanding Your Tax Obligations

The tax obligations for your business will depend on its legal structure, location, and type of industry. However, there are a few common taxes most businesses will face:

Income Taxes: Regardless of your business structure, you'll need to pay taxes on the income your business generates. Sole proprietors and partnerships typically report business income on their personal tax returns. LLCs and corporations may file separate tax returns, depending on how they've chosen to be taxed.

Self-Employment Taxes: If you're a sole proprietor, LLC member, or partner, you'll likely need to pay self-employment taxes on your business income. This covers Social Security and Medicare taxes, which are usually withheld from employees' paychecks, but you'll be responsible for paying these as the business owner.

Sales Tax: If you're selling physical goods or certain services, you may need to collect sales tax from customers. The sales tax rate varies depending on your location, so it's important to check with your state and local tax authority to determine your responsibilities.

Payroll Taxes: If you hire employees, you'll be responsible for withholding and paying payroll taxes. This includes federal and state income taxes, Social Security, Medicare, and unemployment taxes. Be sure to also account for employee benefits like workers' compensation or health insurance if applicable.

2. Setting Up Your Accounting System

To stay on top of your taxes, it's essential to set up a solid accounting system from the get-go. This system will help you track your income, expenses, and deductions, ensuring you're paying the right amount of taxes. Whether you decide to handle your accounting yourself using software like QuickBooks or hire a professional, having an organized system will save you time during tax season and help you avoid costly mistakes.

One crucial part of your accounting system will be keeping track of your deductions. Business expenses like office supplies, travel costs, and marketing expenses can often be deducted from your taxable income, reducing your overall tax liability. Keeping accurate records of all your business expenses is essential for ensuring you claim all the deductions you're entitled to.

3. Filing Your Taxes

The next step is filing your taxes on time. Depending on your business structure, you'll file either as an individual or as a business entity. The IRS has specific forms for different types of businesses, and it's important to make sure you're using the right ones.

Sole Proprietorship: If you're a sole proprietor, you'll file taxes using Schedule C (Profit or Loss from Business), which is attached to your individual tax return (Form 1040).

Partnership: Partnerships must file Form 1065, which reports the partnership's income, deductions, and profits. Each partner will receive a Schedule K-1, which reports their share of the partnership's income.

LLC: The tax filing for an LLC depends on how it's classified for tax purposes. Single-member LLCs are typically taxed as sole proprietors, while multi-member LLCs are taxed as partnerships.

However, LLCs can also elect to be taxed as an S-Corp or C-Corp if it benefits them.

Corporation: Corporations file Form 1120 for C-Corps or Form 1120S for S-Corps.

It's important to keep deadlines in mind to avoid penalties for late filing or payment. The IRS offers tax extensions for businesses, but even if you file for an extension, you'll still need to pay any estimated taxes owed by the original deadline.

4. Working with a Tax Professional

If navigating taxes seems complex, you're not alone. Many entrepreneurs choose to work with a tax professional to ensure they're meeting all their obligations and taking advantage of any tax-saving opportunities. A certified public accountant (CPA) or tax advisor can help you manage your business's taxes, file returns, and provide valuable advice on deductions, credits, and strategies for minimizing taxes.

Conclusion

Registering your business and handling taxes may not be the most glamorous part of entrepreneurship, but they are vital steps in setting up your business for long-term success. By carefully registering your business, choosing the right structure, and staying on top of your tax obligations, you'll protect yourself from legal complications and financial missteps. Taking the time to understand these foundational aspects of business will pay off in the long run, giving you more time and energy to focus on growing and thriving as a business owner. With a strong foundation in place, you're ready to move forward and take your business to new heights.

Setting Up Business Banking and Funding Options: A Crucial Step for Success

When it comes to launching your business, setting up the right banking and funding options can make all the difference. Not only does it provide you with the tools to manage your finances, but it also sets the stage for the growth and stability of your business. Whether you're just starting out or planning to scale, understanding your business banking needs and funding options will help ensure that your business runs smoothly, meets its financial goals, and is ready for any opportunities that come your way.

In this chapter, we'll dive into the importance of business banking and explore the various funding options available to new business owners. From setting up a business bank account to securing financing, we'll guide you through the essential steps to get your business financially organized and ready for success.

Why You Need a Business Bank Account

One of the first things you should do after registering your business is set up a business bank account. Operating your business through a personal account can create confusion, mix your personal and business finances, and complicate tax reporting. Having a separate business account not only makes it easier to manage your business finances but also helps protect your personal assets.

A business account provides several benefits:

Separation of personal and business funds: It keeps your personal finances separate from your business transactions, which is important for legal reasons and accounting clarity. This separation also helps maintain professionalism when dealing with clients and vendors.

Professionalism: Using a business account adds a layer of credibility and professionalism when writing checks, processing payments, and handling business expenses.

Easier tax filing: With a dedicated business account, it's much easier to track expenses, income, and deductions when tax season rolls around, helping you avoid costly mistakes and reducing the likelihood of an audit.

Access to business services: Business accounts often come with additional services, such as merchant processing, business loans, and lines of credit, which can help you grow and manage your business more effectively.

To open a business bank account, you will need to provide documentation like your Employer Identification Number (EIN), business registration, and other proof of your business structure. Shop around for a bank that offers the services and features that match your business's needs, such as low fees, easy online banking, and access to business loans or lines of credit.

Choosing the Right Business Account Features

Once you've selected a bank, the next step is choosing the right type of account for your business. There are several types of accounts you may want to consider:

Business Checking Account: This is the core account for your day-to-day business operations. It allows you to deposit money, pay bills, and process transactions. Some banks offer basic accounts with no monthly fees, while others may have additional features like rewards or higher interest rates.

Business Savings Account: This account is used to set aside money for future expenses, emergencies, or growth. It's a great way to keep your cash flow organized and ensure you have funds available when you need them.

Merchant Services Account: If you plan to accept credit card payments or online payments, you may need a merchant services account. This account allows you to process payments securely, providing a smooth transaction experience for your customers.

Business Credit Card: Having a business credit card helps you manage expenses, build credit for your business, and track purchases more efficiently. It can also provide rewards, cash back, or other incentives, depending on the card you choose.

Understanding Your Funding Options

Once your business banking setup is complete, the next step is to explore the different funding options available to finance your business. Whether you need capital to get started or funding to fuel growth, understanding your choices will help you find the best fit for your needs.

1. Self-Funding (Bootstrapping)

The simplest form of funding is self-funding, also known as bootstrapping. This involves using your own savings, personal assets, or income from other ventures to finance your business. While this method doesn't require you to take on debt or give up equity, it comes with risks—namely, the potential to drain your personal finances if the business doesn't succeed.

Bootstrapping is ideal for businesses that don't need large amounts of capital to get started or those that prefer to retain full control of their business without outside investors. It's also a great way to test your business idea without the pressure of paying back loans or meeting investors' expectations.

2. Business Loans

If you need more substantial funding, a business loan might be the right option. Loans are typically provided by banks, credit unions, or online lenders and come with a fixed interest rate and repayment terms. Business loans can be used for a variety of purposes, from buying equipment to expanding your operations or covering operating expenses.

When applying for a business loan, be prepared to provide detailed information about your business, including your business plan, financial projections, and credit history. Loan options include:

SBA Loans: Loans backed by the Small Business Administration (SBA) are a popular choice because they tend to offer lower interest rates and more favorable terms. However, the application process can be lengthy, and it may be difficult for new businesses to qualify.

Term Loans: These are traditional loans where you borrow a lump sum of money and repay it over a fixed period of time. Term loans can be used for a variety of business needs, but they often require strong credit and financial history.

Lines of Credit: A line of credit is a flexible form of borrowing that allows you to access funds up to a certain limit whenever needed. You only pay interest on the amount you borrow, making it a good option for businesses that experience fluctuating cash flow.

3. Investors and Venture Capital

If your business has significant growth potential, you may want to consider seeking outside investment. Investors can provide capital in exchange for equity (ownership) or convertible debt. This can be a great way to scale your business quickly, but it also means giving up a portion of control and sharing profits with your investors.

Types of investors include:

Angel Investors: These are individual investors who provide early-stage funding in exchange for equity or debt. They often offer mentorship and guidance, along with capital.

Venture Capitalists: Venture capital firms invest in high-growth startups with a lot of potential. They typically focus on businesses in technology, healthcare, or other high-growth sectors. While venture capitalists can provide significant funding, they also require a high level of control and often demand significant equity.

4. Crowdfunding

Another popular option for raising capital is crowdfunding. Websites like Kickstarter, GoFundMe, and Indiegogo allow you to raise funds by appealing directly to a large number of individuals who believe in your business idea. Crowdfunding can be an excellent way to test your business concept, gain visibility, and secure capital without giving up equity or taking on debt.

To succeed with crowdfunding, you'll need a compelling pitch, an engaging story, and a marketing plan to reach potential backers. Be sure to offer attractive rewards or incentives to encourage people to support your project.

5. Grants

For certain types of businesses, there may be grants available to help fund your venture. Government agencies, non-profits, and private organizations offer grants to businesses that meet specific criteria, such as operating in a particular industry or serving underrepresented communities. Grants are highly competitive and usually require detailed proposals, but they can provide non-repayable funding to help you get started.

Conclusion

Setting up business banking and funding options is a vital step in launching and growing your business. A dedicated business bank account will streamline your finances, improve professionalism, and make managing your cash flow easier. When it comes to funding, there are many options available, from self-funding to loans, investors, and crowdfunding. The key is to choose the option that aligns with your business goals, risk tolerance, and long-term vision. By getting your banking and funding set up properly from the start, you'll lay a strong foundation for your business's financial success, allowing you to focus on growing and achieving your entrepreneurial dreams.

Chapter 5:

Marketing Made Simple: Reaching Your Audience

Marketing is the bridge between your business and your customers. It's how you make people aware of your products or services, communicate your value, and convince them to take action. But with so many marketing strategies, channels, and tools available today, the process can sometimes feel overwhelming. How do you know which approach is right for your business? How do you get the attention of your audience and keep them engaged?

In this chapter, we'll break down the essentials of effective marketing—making it simple, actionable, and fun. We'll cover how to define your target audience, choose the right marketing channels, and create compelling messages that resonate with your customers. Whether you're just starting or looking to refine your marketing efforts, this guide will help you master the basics of reaching your audience and turning them into loyal customers.

Defining Your Target Audience

The first step in any successful marketing strategy is understanding your audience. After all, you can't effectively market your products or services if you don't know who you're speaking to. Defining your target audience is essential for creating tailored marketing campaigns that speak directly to the people most likely to purchase from you.

Start by creating a buyer persona. This is a detailed, semi-fictional representation of your ideal customer. Consider factors such as:

Demographics: Age, gender, income level, education, job title, and location.

Psychographics: Interests, values, hobbies, and lifestyle choices.

Pain points: What problems are they facing that your product or service can solve?

Buying behavior: What influences their purchasing decisions? Are they price-sensitive, or do they value quality over cost?

Once you have a clear understanding of your audience, you'll be able to craft marketing messages that speak directly to their needs and desires. This ensures that your marketing efforts are more likely to resonate, leading to higher engagement and conversions.

Crafting a Strong Value Proposition

With a clear understanding of your audience, the next step is to articulate your value proposition—a statement that explains why your product or service is the best solution to your customers' problems. A strong value proposition should highlight the unique benefits of your offering and communicate how it will improve your customers' lives.

Think about your business from your customers' perspective. What makes you stand out from your competitors? What problem do you solve better than anyone else? Be sure to express this in simple, clear language that resonates with your audience's pain points and aspirations. Whether it's faster delivery, superior quality, or innovative features, your value proposition should be the foundation of all your marketing communications.

Choosing the Right Marketing Channels

In today's digital world, there are countless marketing channels available, and it can be tempting to try and be everywhere at once. However, not all channels will be suitable for your business, and spreading yourself too thin can be counterproductive. To reach your audience effectively, it's important to choose the marketing channels that align with where your target audience spends their time and how they prefer to receive information.

Here are some of the most common marketing channels to consider:

Social Media: Platforms like Facebook, Instagram, Twitter, LinkedIn, and TikTok are excellent for building a community, engaging with your audience, and driving brand awareness. Social media is particularly useful for businesses in industries like fashion, food, health, and beauty, where visual content and direct interaction are key to success.

Email Marketing: Despite the rise of social media, email marketing remains one of the most effective ways to reach your audience. It allows you to nurture relationships with customers over time, provide value through personalized messages, and promote products directly to an engaged audience. Building an email list early on is a smart way to keep your audience informed and loyal.

Search Engine Optimization (SEO): SEO is the practice of optimizing your website to rank higher in search engine results, making it easier for customers to find you. This involves using relevant keywords, creating high-quality content, and ensuring your website is user-friendly. A solid SEO strategy helps you attract organic traffic and build trust with potential customers.

Paid Advertising: If you have the budget for it, paid ads can be an excellent way to get immediate visibility. Whether through Google Ads, Facebook ads, or influencer marketing, paid advertising allows you to target specific demographics and drive traffic to your site. However, it's important to track your ROI and optimize your campaigns to ensure they're delivering results.

Content Marketing: Content marketing involves creating valuable, informative content that educates and engages your audience. This could be in the form of blog posts, videos, infographics, or podcasts. By providing helpful content, you position your business as an expert in your industry, build trust, and create lasting relationships with your customers.

Public Relations (PR): Building relationships with the media and gaining press coverage can boost your credibility and reach a wider audience. PR involves sending press releases, collaborating with influencers, and positioning yourself as a thought leader in your field. It's a great way to build your brand's reputation and credibility.

Building a Marketing Plan

Once you've identified your audience, value proposition, and marketing channels, it's time to develop a marketing plan. This plan will serve as your roadmap for executing your strategy and tracking your results. A good marketing plan should include the following elements:

Goals and Objectives: What do you want to achieve with your marketing efforts? Are you looking to increase brand awareness, drive traffic to your website, or generate sales? Set clear, measurable goals that align with your business objectives.

Budget: Determine how much money you can allocate to your marketing efforts. Be realistic about what you can afford and prioritize channels that will give you the best return on investment.

Content Calendar: Plan out your content in advance to ensure consistency. A content calendar will help you stay organized and make sure you're regularly engaging with your audience. Include blog posts, social media updates, email campaigns, and any other content you plan to create.

Metrics and Analytics: Track your progress by using analytics tools to measure the effectiveness of your marketing campaigns. Google Analytics, social media insights, and email performance metrics can help you assess what's working and what's not. This data will guide future marketing decisions and ensure you're continuously improving.

Engaging Your Audience

Marketing isn't just about pushing your product; it's about creating relationships and engaging with your audience. Interaction and engagement are key to building trust and loyalty, and they can help turn one-time buyers into repeat customers and brand advocates.

Here are a few ways to engage your audience:

Respond to Comments: Whether it's on social media, blog posts, or emails, always take the time to respond to your customers. Show that you care about their feedback and concerns.

Personalization: Use your customer data to personalize your marketing messages. Personalized emails, special offers, and targeted ads are more likely to resonate with your audience and lead to conversions.

Run Contests and Giveaways: People love free stuff, so running a contest or giveaway is a great way to engage your audience and create excitement around your brand. Just be sure to make the rules clear and follow through on your promises.

Share User-Generated Content: Encourage your customers to share their experiences with your product or service. Sharing user-generated content not only helps you build social proof but also strengthens the connection between your brand and your audience.

Conclusion

Marketing doesn't have to be complicated. By understanding your audience, crafting a strong value proposition, and choosing the right channels, you can create a marketing strategy that helps your business stand out and grow. With a solid marketing plan in place and a focus on engagement, you'll be able to reach your target customers, build lasting relationships, and ultimately drive success. Remember, marketing is an ongoing process, so keep refining your approach, measuring results, and adapting to new trends. The more you engage with your audience, the more your business will thrive.

Understanding Your Target Audience: The Key to Successful Marketing

One of the most crucial steps in building a successful business is understanding your target audience. Without a clear picture of who your customers are, your marketing efforts will lack focus and direction. It's like trying to hit a moving target in the dark—you may get lucky once in a while, but more often than not, you'll miss the mark. However, when you understand your target audience deeply, you're able to tailor your messaging, products, and services to meet their exact needs, creating a stronger connection and more effective business growth.

In this chapter, we'll explore how to define and understand your target audience so you can make smarter marketing decisions. From identifying key characteristics to analyzing their behavior, we'll dive into practical strategies that will empower you to connect with the people who matter most to your business.

The Importance of Knowing Your Target Audience

Understanding your target audience goes beyond knowing who might buy your product. It's about getting into their minds, understanding their pain points, aspirations, habits, and desires. The more you know about your customers, the better you can serve them and stand out from your competitors.

When you understand your target audience, you can:

Create tailored marketing messages: Knowing what motivates your customers allows you to craft marketing messages that speak directly to their needs, desires, and values.

Choose the right channels: Every audience has preferred ways of consuming content, whether it's through social media, blogs, email newsletters, or in-person interactions. Understanding these preferences helps you reach your customers in the most effective way possible.

Develop products they want: By analyzing your audience's pain points and needs, you can create products or services that truly solve their problems, making your offerings more appealing and valuable.

Build stronger relationships: Customers are more likely to trust and stay loyal to a brand that understands them. When you show that you truly get them, it fosters long-term relationships.

Identifying Key Characteristics of Your Target Audience

To start understanding your target audience, you first need to gather key demographic and psychographic information. This data will help you paint a clear picture of who your ideal customers are and what drives them.

Demographics: These are the basic, measurable characteristics of your audience. Demographics include:

Age: Are your customers young adults, middle-aged professionals, or seniors? Different age groups have different priorities and preferences.

Gender: Gender can influence product preferences, shopping habits, and marketing language. Consider whether your product appeals to a particular gender or if it's gender-neutral.

Income level: Knowing the income range of your audience helps you determine pricing strategies and the kind of products they might be interested in.

Location: Are you targeting a local audience, a specific country, or a global market? The location of your audience affects logistics, language, cultural preferences, and market demand.

Education and job title: These factors can help you understand your audience's interests and the language they use. For instance, marketing to a highly educated audience might require a different tone and approach than marketing to a general public.

Psychographics: While demographics tell you who your audience is, psychographics give you a deeper understanding of why they behave the way they do. Psychographic data includes:

Lifestyle: What do your customers do in their free time? What are their hobbies, interests, and values? For example, a business catering to outdoor enthusiasts might focus on nature, sustainability, and adventure in its marketing.

Personality traits: Are your customers extroverts who love socializing, or introverts who prefer quiet and solitude? Tailoring your messaging to fit their personalities can increase your appeal.

Values and beliefs: What's important to your audience? Whether it's environmental sustainability, social justice, or health and wellness, aligning your business with their values creates stronger connections.

Behavioral triggers: What drives your audience to make a purchase? Are they motivated by convenience, price, luxury, or status? Understanding these triggers helps you craft compelling offers that resonate deeply.

Tools and Methods for Gathering Audience Insights

Once you've identified the key characteristics of your target audience, the next step is to gather data that will help you refine your understanding. Here are some tools and methods you can use to collect valuable insights:

Customer Surveys: Surveys are one of the best ways to gather direct feedback from your audience. By asking questions about their preferences, pain points, and purchasing habits, you can gain valuable insights that will guide your marketing efforts. Tools like SurveyMonkey or Google Forms can help you easily create and distribute surveys.

Social Media Analytics: Social media platforms like Facebook, Instagram, and Twitter offer robust analytics that reveal important information about your audience's age, gender, location, and interests.

These insights can help you refine your messaging and content strategy to better match their preferences.

Website Analytics: Using tools like Google Analytics, you can track how visitors interact with your website. This includes the pages they visit, how long they stay, and where they're coming from. By analyzing these patterns, you can identify your most engaged visitors and refine your content and offerings to appeal to them.

Customer Interviews: While surveys provide quantitative data, customer interviews allow for deeper, qualitative insights. Speaking directly to your customers helps you understand their emotions, motivations, and pain points in their own words. You can conduct interviews via phone, video calls, or even in person.

Competitor Analysis: Analyzing your competitors can help you understand the audience they're targeting and what works for them. Look at their marketing tactics, customer reviews, and social media presence. Identify gaps or opportunities where you can differentiate your brand.

Segmenting Your Audience

Once you have a clearer picture of who your target audience is, it's time to consider segmentation. Not all customers are the same, and grouping them into different segments based on shared characteristics allows you to create more personalized and relevant marketing strategies.

Common ways to segment your audience include:

Demographic segmentation: Grouping customers by age, gender, income level, or other basic characteristics.

Geographic segmentation: Grouping customers by location—whether by country, state, city, or neighborhood.

Behavioral segmentation: Segmenting based on customer behavior, such as purchase history, brand loyalty, or product usage.

Psychographic segmentation: Grouping customers based on shared values, interests, or lifestyle.

By segmenting your audience, you can create tailored messages, offers, and content that are more likely to resonate with each group, increasing your chances of conversion.

Using Audience Insights to Shape Your Marketing Strategy

Once you've gathered insights into your target audience, the next step is to apply that knowledge to your marketing strategy. A deeper understanding of your audience should influence:

Product development: Ensure your products and services meet the specific needs and desires of your target audience. If you understand their pain points, you can create solutions that address those needs directly.

Brand positioning: Your brand's image and messaging should align with the values and personality traits of your audience. If you're targeting a younger, trendier demographic, your brand's tone and aesthetic should reflect that.

Content creation: The content you create, whether blog posts, social media updates, or videos, should be designed with your audience's preferences in mind. Create content that educates, entertains, or solves problems for them.

Advertising and promotions: Use the data you've gathered to determine where and how to advertise your product. Knowing your audience's preferences for social media, email, or even offline channels can help you choose the best platforms for your ads.

Conclusion

Understanding your target audience is the foundation of successful marketing. When you know who your customers are, what they want, and how they behave, you can tailor every aspect of your marketing to resonate with them. By gathering data, analyzing your audience's preferences, and segmenting them into actionable groups, you can create marketing strategies that not only reach the right people but also drive real, lasting results. The more you understand your audience, the more effectively you can meet their needs and build a loyal customer base.

Branding Basics and Creating a Unique Value Proposition

Branding is much more than just a logo or a catchy tagline—it's the entire experience your customers have with your business. It's the way your business feels, how it's perceived, and the promise it delivers. Strong branding sets you apart in a crowded market, builds trust, and helps establish long-term relationships with your customers. Whether you're launching a new business or refreshing an existing one, understanding the fundamentals of branding and crafting a unique value proposition (UVP) are essential for standing out and driving success.

In this chapter, we'll explore the key components of branding and guide you through the process of developing a UVP that resonates with your target audience. From defining your brand identity to communicating your brand promise effectively, we'll break it all down to make it simple, practical, and impactful.

What is Branding?

Branding is the process of creating a distinct and memorable identity for your business. It encompasses everything that makes your business unique—from your visual elements (such as your logo, colors, and fonts) to your messaging, customer service, and overall customer experience.

Think of branding as the personality of your business. It's how your customers feel when they interact with you, what they associate with your business, and the emotional connection they have with your brand.

Your branding should tell a compelling story that connects with your audience on a deeper level. It's the promise you make to your customers about the value you will deliver. When done well, branding can build loyalty, increase customer retention, and give you a competitive edge.

The key components of branding include:

Brand Identity: The visual elements that represent your brand, including your logo, color palette, typography, and imagery. These elements help create recognition and consistency across all your marketing materials.

Brand Voice and Messaging: The tone and language you use to communicate with your audience. Your brand voice should reflect your company's values and resonate with your target audience's emotions and needs.

Customer Experience: Every interaction your customers have with your business, from browsing your website to making a purchase and receiving customer support. A positive experience reinforces your brand's promise and strengthens customer loyalty.

Brand Positioning: The place your brand occupies in the market relative to your competitors. Brand positioning defines how you want your audience to perceive you and what makes you different.

The Power of a Unique Value Proposition (UVP)

A Unique Value Proposition (UVP) is the core of your branding. It's a clear, concise statement that explains the unique benefits your business offers to customers and why they should choose you over the competition. Your UVP should highlight what sets you apart and address your customers' most pressing needs, desires, or pain points.

Think of your UVP as a promise to your customers: "Here's how we're going to make your life better or easier, and here's why we're the best at it." It should answer the fundamental question in your customer's mind: "What's in it for me?"

A strong UVP is:

Clear and concise: It should be easy to understand and communicate in just a few sentences.

Customer-centric: It focuses on the value and benefits your customers will receive, not just the features of your product or service.

Differentiating: It explains why you're different from your competitors and why that difference matters.

Compelling: It motivates customers to take action by addressing their needs, desires, or pain points.

Steps to Create a Unique Value Proposition

1. Understand Your Customers' Needs: The first step in crafting a UVP is understanding your customers' pain points, challenges, and desires. What problems are they facing, and how can your product or service solve them? Your UVP should speak directly to these needs. Conduct surveys, read customer reviews, and engage with your audience to gain insights into what matters most to them.

2. Analyze Your Competitors: Take a look at what your competitors are offering and identify any gaps or areas where you can do things better. Your UVP should highlight what sets you apart from the competition. For example, if your competitors focus on speed, perhaps you can emphasize quality or customer service as your unique advantage.

3. Define Your Brand Promise: Your UVP should reflect the promise you're making to your customers. What are you offering that others aren't? This could be a unique feature of your product, an exceptional customer experience, or a particular benefit that your audience values. Your promise should align with your brand values and be something that you can consistently deliver on.

4. Be Specific: Vagueness doesn't sell. Instead of saying "We offer great customer service," explain how your customer service is different and better than your competitors. For example, "Our customer service team is available 24/7 to provide instant support, ensuring you never have to wait for

assistance." Specificity creates trust and makes your UVP more memorable.

5. Keep It Simple: A UVP should be easy to understand and communicate. Avoid jargon and complex language—get straight to the point. A good UVP can be shared in a single sentence or two, and it should immediately convey the unique benefit of your business in a way that resonates with your target audience.

6. Test and Refine: Once you've developed your UVP, test it with your target audience to see if it resonates. Does it clearly convey the unique value you're offering? Is it compelling enough to prompt action? Get feedback from customers, team members, and industry experts, and make adjustments as needed.

Examples of Strong UVPs

To help you visualize what a strong UVP looks like in action, let's look at a few real-world examples:

Apple: "Think Different." Apple's UVP emphasizes its innovative approach and high-quality products, distinguishing itself from competitors who offer more generic technology. The focus is on providing a unique, high-end experience that appeals to people who value design, performance, and creativity.

FedEx: "When it absolutely, positively has to be there overnight." FedEx's UVP focuses on reliability and speed, reassuring customers that their packages will be delivered on time, no matter what. This message speaks directly to customers' need for trust and dependability.

Dollar Shave Club: "A great shave for a few bucks a month." Dollar Shave Club's UVP is simple, cost-effective, and speaks directly to people looking for affordable convenience. It cuts through the noise of traditional razor brands by offering a subscription service that delivers high-quality razors directly to customers' doors.

How Branding and Your UVP Work Together

Branding and your UVP are intertwined—one supports the other. Your UVP communicates the unique value your business offers, while your branding helps you deliver that promise in a compelling way. Together, they create a consistent and powerful message that resonates with your audience.

For example, if your UVP is based on delivering exceptional customer service, your branding should reflect that promise. This could include a friendly and approachable tone in your marketing materials, easy-to-navigate customer support channels, and prompt follow-up emails. Every touchpoint with your customers should reinforce the brand promise your UVP communicates.

Conclusion

Building a strong brand starts with understanding your audience and delivering a clear, compelling value proposition. By developing a unique value proposition that speaks directly to your customers' needs, desires, and pain points, you can differentiate your business and stand out in a crowded marketplace. Pairing your UVP with a well-crafted brand identity will help you create lasting connections with your customers, build trust, and drive long-term success. Keep refining your brand and UVP as your business grows, and always stay focused on the value you're offering—because at the end of the day, it's all about giving your customers something they can't find anywhere else.

Effective Low-Cost Marketing Strategies for Small Businesses

For small businesses, marketing often presents a significant challenge, particularly when operating with limited budgets. Effective marketing strategies are essential to drive growth, build brand awareness, and attract customers without overspending. Several low-cost marketing approaches can yield significant results when executed strategically. This section will outline proven, cost-efficient marketing strategies that small businesses can implement to maximize their marketing efforts while minimizing expenses.

1. Social Media Marketing

Social media platforms provide an invaluable tool for reaching a broad audience without incurring substantial costs. These platforms allow businesses to engage with potential customers, build relationships, and promote products or services.

Organic Social Media Content: Posting regularly on platforms such as Facebook, Instagram, Twitter, and LinkedIn can help businesses connect with their audience directly. The key to success lies in consistency, relevance, and creativity. By sharing valuable content that aligns with the interests of the target audience—whether through informative blog posts, product updates, or behind-the-scenes looks at the business—small businesses can generate organic engagement without spending money on ads.

Community Building: Creating a loyal online community around a brand helps build trust and fosters word-of-mouth marketing. Small businesses can use social media to engage with followers by responding to comments, asking questions, and encouraging discussions. This helps enhance the brand's presence and facilitates customer loyalty.

Influencer Partnerships: Partnering with micro-influencers who have a smaller but highly engaged following can provide cost-effective promotional opportunities. Micro-influencers often charge less than larger influencers, yet their followers tend to trust their recommendations, leading to higher engagement and conversion rates.

2. Content Marketing

Content marketing is a highly effective, low-cost strategy for businesses to generate leads and engage with potential customers. This involves creating valuable, relevant content designed to attract, inform, and nurture an audience. Content marketing efforts can include blogs, videos, podcasts, or infographics, depending on the business type and audience preferences.

Blogging: Creating a blog on the company website and posting regularly can drive organic traffic from search engines. By focusing on topics that address customers' questions or solve their problems, businesses can build authority in their industry and attract more visitors over time. Additionally, blog posts can be shared on social media to further expand reach.

Video Content: Video content, such as product demonstrations or how-to videos, is particularly effective on social media platforms. With tools like YouTube or Facebook Live, businesses can create video content that resonates with their audience. Producing high-quality videos doesn't require expensive equipment; smartphones and free editing software can often suffice.

SEO (Search Engine Optimization): Effective content marketing must be paired with SEO techniques to ensure that it reaches the right audience. By optimizing blog posts, videos, and other content with relevant keywords, small businesses can improve their visibility on search engines like Google without having to pay for advertising.

3. Email Marketing

Email marketing remains one of the most cost-effective and high-return marketing strategies. By collecting email addresses through opt-ins on your website, social media platforms, or in-store sign-ups, businesses can create a direct communication channel with customers.

Newsletters: Regular email newsletters that provide valuable content, special offers, or company updates keep customers informed and engaged. Personalizing these emails based on customer preferences or past purchases can increase their relevance and improve engagement rates.

Automation: Email automation tools, such as Mailchimp or ConvertKit, allow businesses to set up automated email campaigns. These can be triggered by actions like signing up for a newsletter, making a purchase, or abandoning a shopping cart. Automation helps businesses maintain ongoing communication with customers without dedicating additional resources.

Segmentation: Segmenting email lists based on customer demographics, behaviors, or preferences enables businesses to send targeted content, improving the chances of conversions. For example, sending a promotional offer to customers who have previously purchased similar products may lead to higher sales.

4. Referral Programs

Referral marketing leverages existing customers to bring in new business. This strategy is built on the premise that people are more likely to trust recommendations from family, friends, or acquaintances than traditional advertising. Referral programs incentivize current customers to refer new customers, benefiting both the referrer and the referred.

Incentivizing Referrals: Offering discounts, free products, or other rewards for successful referrals encourages customers to share their positive experiences. The key to success with referral programs is ensuring the reward is compelling enough to motivate action without eating into profits excessively.

Tracking Referrals: Using referral program software (e.g., ReferralCandy, Yotpo) allows businesses to track and manage referral activity easily. This technology simplifies the process of rewarding customers and provides insights into the program's effectiveness.

5. Partnerships and Collaborations

Small businesses can also benefit from collaborating with other local businesses or complementary brands. Such partnerships can lead to cross-promotions that expose both brands to new audiences without incurring significant costs.

Cross-Promotions: Collaborating with businesses that share a similar customer base but are not direct competitors can be mutually beneficial. For example, a coffee shop may partner with a local bakery to offer joint discounts or bundled products. These efforts help expand visibility while maintaining low marketing costs.

Event Sponsorships: Small businesses can sponsor local events, charity functions, or community gatherings in exchange for branding opportunities. Although some events may charge sponsorship fees, they often come at a fraction of the cost of traditional advertising. In addition, businesses gain exposure to a targeted audience that is likely to be interested in their products or services.

6. Guerrilla Marketing

Guerrilla marketing involves creative, unconventional marketing tactics designed to generate buzz with minimal expense. This approach often uses bold, eye-catching, and attention-grabbing methods to create memorable impressions.

Street Art or Public Installations: Creative public displays, like chalk drawings, posters, or flash mobs, can help draw attention to your business without requiring a substantial budget. Guerrilla marketing is effective because it focuses on surprise and novelty, which can go viral through social media.

Viral Campaigns: Creating shareable content that has the potential to go viral, such as funny memes, contests, or challenges, can increase brand awareness at a minimal cost. While viral campaigns are unpredictable, businesses can use their understanding of their target audience to create content that resonates and encourages sharing.

7. Networking and Community Engagement

Building strong relationships within your local community or industry can be an effective, low-cost way to market your business. Networking allows you to increase word-of-mouth referrals and establish a reputation as an engaged, supportive member of the community.

Attend Local Events: Participating in or sponsoring local events, such as farmers markets, fairs, or trade shows, can help businesses meet potential customers face-to-face. Even if the event is low-cost or free, the exposure can lead to direct sales and lasting relationships.

Online Communities and Forums: Engaging with niche online communities or industry-specific forums allows businesses to connect with potential customers by providing value, answering questions, or sharing expert knowledge. This strategy helps businesses establish credibility and authority within their field.

Conclusion

Effective low-cost marketing strategies focus on leveraging creativity, digital tools, and existing customer relationships to drive growth and visibility. By utilizing social media, content marketing, email marketing, referral programs, partnerships, guerrilla marketing, and networking, small businesses can reach a wide audience and achieve significant results without requiring large marketing budgets. The key to success lies in consistency, strategic planning, and a deep understanding of the target audience. With these low-cost strategies in place, businesses can compete effectively and build a strong, sustainable brand.

Chapter 6:

Harnessing Technology: Tools and Platforms for Growth

In today's fast-paced, digitally driven world, technology plays a critical role in transforming businesses and driving growth. For small businesses and entrepreneurs, embracing the right technology isn't just a convenience—it's a necessity. With the right tools at your disposal, you can streamline processes, enhance customer engagement, and scale faster than ever before. But with so many options available, how do you choose the ones that will work best for you? In this chapter, we'll dive into some essential tools and platforms that can help propel your business forward by harnessing the power of technology.

1. Project Management Tools: Organize for Success

When you're running a business, staying organized is key to ensuring that everything gets done efficiently. Project management tools help you keep track of tasks, deadlines, and progress, making sure nothing falls through the cracks. Whether you're a solo entrepreneur or leading a team, these tools can keep everyone on the same page and help you achieve your goals.

Trello is a popular choice for visual thinkers, offering a card and board system that allows you to organize projects and tasks. It's ideal for tracking tasks in a simple, drag-and-drop format, making it easy to assign tasks, set deadlines, and monitor progress.

Asana is another fantastic tool for businesses looking for more structure and robust features. It allows you to track complex projects, assign subtasks, and create timelines. Its ability to integrate with other tools like Slack and Google Drive makes it a versatile choice for teams.

Monday.com offers a highly customizable experience that lets you tailor workflows to your exact needs. With intuitive visuals and a wide range of templates, Monday.com can be adapted to a variety of industries, making it a great all-around tool for business organization.

The right project management software can save you time, increase efficiency, and help you stay focused on what really matters—growing your business.

2. Communication Platforms: Stay Connected

Effective communication is the foundation of any successful business. Whether you're working with a remote team, managing customer inquiries, or collaborating with partners, having the right communication tools is crucial.

Slack has revolutionized team communication with its channels, allowing you to organize conversations by topic, department, or project. It's an excellent tool for collaboration, file sharing, and real-time communication, ensuring that everyone stays informed.

Zoom remains the go-to platform for virtual meetings. With video conferencing, screen-sharing capabilities, and even webinar hosting, Zoom makes it easy to connect with your team, clients, and prospects no matter where you are.

Microsoft Teams integrates seamlessly with Office 365, making it perfect for businesses that already use Microsoft tools. Teams combines messaging, video calls, file sharing, and project collaboration into one unified platform, making it a great choice for businesses that need a comprehensive communication solution.

These communication tools empower you to stay connected, whether you're in the same office or working from opposite sides of the world. With the right platforms, you can foster stronger relationships and keep the wheels of your business turning smoothly.

3. Customer Relationship Management (CRM) Tools: Build Lasting Connections

Building strong relationships with your customers is crucial for sustained growth. CRM tools help you track interactions, understand customer behavior, and offer personalized experiences that foster loyalty.

HubSpot CRM is a great starting point for small businesses. With its free version, you can manage contacts, track sales, and monitor customer interactions. It's user-friendly and integrates well with a range of other tools, making it a fantastic entry point for businesses just starting with CRM.

Salesforce is one of the most powerful CRM platforms available, known for its scalability and extensive features. If you're looking for a robust system that allows for custom reporting, automation, and detailed customer insights, Salesforce is a go-to solution. Although it may be more suitable for larger businesses, it can scale with your company as you grow.

Zoho CRM offers a flexible and affordable CRM solution that works for businesses of all sizes. It comes with features like lead management, workflow automation, and email marketing, allowing you to optimize your sales processes and enhance customer relationships.

With the right CRM system in place, you can gain deeper insights into your customers' needs, improve communication, and ultimately drive more sales by offering personalized experiences that resonate.

4. Marketing Automation: Streamline Your Efforts

Marketing automation tools help you save time by automating repetitive tasks such as email campaigns, social media posting, and customer follow-ups. With automation, you can create personalized marketing experiences that nurture leads and convert them into customers—all while freeing up your time to focus on other important aspects of your business.

Mailchimp is one of the most popular email marketing tools, known for its user-friendly interface and powerful automation features. With Mailchimp, you can create custom email campaigns, track performance, and even segment your audience to ensure you're sending the right message to the right people.

ActiveCampaign is another excellent tool for marketing automation, offering email marketing, CRM, and sales automation all in one platform. It's ideal for businesses that want to manage and automate their entire customer journey, from lead generation to sales.

ConvertKit is particularly useful for content creators, bloggers, and small businesses that want a simple, intuitive email marketing solution. It offers great automation features and allows you to build email sequences that nurture leads over time.

By using marketing automation tools, you can deliver timely, relevant content to your audience without needing to handle everything manually. This means your marketing efforts are more consistent and can generate greater results with less effort.

5. Accounting and Financial Management: Stay on Top of Your Finances

Financial management is at the core of every business, and using the right tools can help you keep everything organized, from bookkeeping to invoicing to tax preparation. Proper financial management ensures you stay on top of your cash flow and make informed decisions for the future.

QuickBooks is an industry leader in accounting software. With features such as invoicing, expense tracking, payroll management, and tax calculation, QuickBooks provides everything you need to manage your business finances. It's easy to use and perfect for small businesses that need a reliable accounting solution.

Wave is a free accounting software option that offers features like invoicing, expense tracking, and receipt scanning. It's a great choice for entrepreneurs who want a no-cost solution to manage their finances without sacrificing key features.

Xero is a cloud-based accounting platform that makes it easy to manage finances, track expenses, and generate reports. With its user-friendly interface and robust reporting capabilities, Xero is an excellent option for businesses looking for flexibility and scalability.

The right accounting software allows you to stay on top of your finances, track income and expenses, and prepare for taxes, all while ensuring that your business runs smoothly and efficiently.

6. E-Commerce Platforms: Expand Your Reach

If you sell products, having a user-friendly e-commerce platform is crucial for reaching customers online. Whether you're starting small or aiming to scale your online store, there are several platforms that cater to businesses of all sizes.

Shopify is a go-to solution for e-commerce businesses. It offers customizable templates, integrated payment systems, inventory management, and marketing tools—all within an easy-to-use platform. Shopify is ideal for businesses looking to scale quickly and efficiently.

WooCommerce is a WordPress plugin that allows you to transform your website into an online store. It's affordable and easy to set up, making it perfect for small businesses that want to sell products online without breaking the bank.

BigCommerce provides an all-in-one e-commerce solution with robust features, including SEO optimization, inventory management, and multi-channel selling. It's ideal for businesses that are looking for more advanced features as they grow.

These e-commerce platforms empower businesses to reach a wider audience, streamline the buying process, and scale without the need for complex systems.

Conclusion: Embrace Technology for Sustainable Growth

Technology has the power to transform how businesses operate and grow. By leveraging the right tools and platforms, small business owners can save time, enhance efficiency, improve customer experiences, and ultimately scale their operations. The key is choosing the right technology that aligns with your business needs and goals. With the right mix of project management, communication, marketing, financial, and e-commerce tools, you can set your business up for long-term success. Technology doesn't just support growth—it drives it, and embracing it will give your business the competitive edge it needs to succeed in today's digital age.

Essential Tools for Startups

Starting a business is an exhilarating yet challenging journey, and one of the most important decisions you'll make is choosing the right tools to help streamline your operations. In today's fast-paced world, technology offers a multitude of solutions to help startups stay organized, manage finances, reach customers, and scale operations. The right mix of tools can significantly impact the efficiency and growth of your business. Whether you're a solopreneur or leading a small team, here are some essential tools that every startup needs to thrive in today's competitive market.

1. Project Management Tools: Keep Your Team Organized

At the core of every startup is a group of motivated individuals working toward a common goal. To ensure that everyone is on the same page, effective project management tools are essential. These tools help you stay organized, monitor progress, assign tasks, and meet deadlines, all while fostering collaboration.

Trello is a visually appealing project management tool that uses boards, lists, and cards to organize tasks. Its simple interface allows teams to collaborate on projects, track progress, and make adjustments in real-time. It's an excellent option for startups that need a flexible and easy-to-use tool.

Asana offers a more comprehensive approach to project management, with features like task assignments, timelines, and reporting. Asana is great for managing both large and small projects, making it perfect for teams that are juggling multiple tasks at once.

Basecamp is known for its simplicity and ease of use, offering features such as to-do lists, file sharing, and team messaging. It's an excellent tool for startups that want to keep things simple and organized without overwhelming team members with too many features.

By implementing one of these tools, startups can keep projects on track, increase productivity, and improve communication among team members.

2. Communication Tools: Foster Clear, Consistent Communication

Effective communication is vital to the success of any startup. Whether you're coordinating with your team, communicating with clients, or dealing with suppliers, you need tools that enable seamless communication.

Slack is a team communication tool that allows you to create channels for different topics, projects, or departments. Slack enables real-time messaging, file sharing, and integration with other tools, making it ideal for keeping your team connected, especially if you have remote workers.

Zoom has become the go-to platform for video conferencing. Whether you're hosting virtual meetings, pitching to investors, or collaborating with partners, Zoom makes it easy to communicate face-to-face, share screens, and record meetings for later reference.

Google Meet is another popular video conferencing tool, integrated with Google Workspace. It's perfect for startups already using Google products, providing a seamless experience for video calls, calendar scheduling, and document collaboration.

These communication tools ensure that everyone stays informed and connected, regardless of location or time zone, helping to keep your startup running smoothly.

3. Financial Management Tools: Stay on Top of Your Finances

Managing your finances is crucial when running a startup. You need to track income, expenses, taxes, and budgets, all while ensuring you're making sound financial decisions. Financial management tools simplify these tasks and help you stay on top of your finances.

QuickBooks is one of the most popular accounting software options for startups. It offers features like invoicing, expense tracking, payroll management, and tax calculations. With its intuitive interface and powerful features, QuickBooks makes it easy to manage your startup's finances, even if you don't have a background in accounting.

Wave is a free accounting tool designed for small businesses and startups. It provides features such as invoicing, expense tracking, and receipt scanning, helping entrepreneurs manage their finances without breaking the bank.

FreshBooks is another great accounting software for startups, offering easy-to-use tools for invoicing, time tracking, and project management. FreshBooks is ideal for service-based businesses and entrepreneurs who need an affordable and efficient way to manage their finances.

By utilizing financial management tools, startups can ensure that their money is being spent wisely, helping them to grow without the risk of running into financial trouble.

4. Marketing Tools: Build Your Brand and Reach Customers

Marketing is a cornerstone of any successful startup. With the right tools, you can build your brand, engage your audience, and increase sales. From social media management to email marketing, these tools can help you establish a strong online presence and attract customers.

Mailchimp is one of the most well-known email marketing platforms. It allows you to create customized email campaigns, segment your audience, and track performance. It also offers automation features, so you can send personalized emails based on user actions.

Canva is a powerful design tool that allows you to create stunning visuals for social media, websites, and print materials. Its user-friendly interface and vast library of templates make it ideal for startups with limited design resources.

Hootsuite is a social media management tool that allows you to schedule posts, track engagement, and analyze performance across multiple platforms. By automating social media tasks, Hootsuite saves you time and ensures that you stay consistent with your content.

Google Analytics is a must-have for any startup that has a website. It provides detailed insights into website traffic, user behavior, and conversion rates, allowing you to track the effectiveness of your marketing efforts and make data-driven decisions.

With these marketing tools, startups can efficiently manage campaigns, engage their target audience, and optimize their marketing efforts for maximum impact.

5. Customer Relationship Management (CRM) Tools: Nurture Your Leads

Building strong, lasting relationships with customers is crucial for the long-term success of any startup. CRM tools help you track interactions, manage leads, and improve customer service.

HubSpot CRM is a free, user-friendly CRM platform that helps you track contacts, manage sales pipelines, and measure performance. It integrates well with email and marketing tools, making it a great option for startups looking to grow their customer base.

Salesforce is one of the most comprehensive CRM tools available. It offers features such as lead management, reporting, and automation, making it ideal for startups that want to scale their customer management efforts as they grow.

Zoho CRM is an affordable and customizable CRM solution that includes lead tracking, sales automation, and analytics. It's perfect for startups that need a flexible CRM tool to fit their specific needs.

By using CRM tools, startups can manage customer relationships more effectively, leading to higher satisfaction, increased loyalty, and ultimately, more sales.

6. E-Commerce Tools: Sell Products Online

If your startup involves selling physical or digital products, e-commerce tools are essential for setting up an online store. These platforms allow you to manage inventory, process payments, and deliver a seamless shopping experience for your customers.

Shopify is one of the most popular e-commerce platforms for startups. It offers everything you need to create an online store, including customizable templates, secure payment processing, and inventory management. Shopify is designed for ease of use, making it perfect for entrepreneurs who want to start selling quickly.

WooCommerce is a free WordPress plugin that allows you to turn your website into a fully functional online store. It's ideal for startups that already use WordPress and want an affordable solution for selling products online.

BigCommerce is another powerful e-commerce platform designed for startups. It offers features like multi-channel selling, SEO optimization, and inventory management, making it easy for businesses to scale and reach more customers.

E-commerce tools are a must for any startup selling products online, enabling you to efficiently manage your store and provide an excellent customer experience.

Conclusion: Tools Are Key to Startup Success

The right tools can make a world of difference for your startup. By using a combination of project management, communication, financial management, marketing, CRM, and e-commerce tools, you can streamline your operations, stay organized, and focus on growing your business. With technology at your side, you'll have the support you need to overcome challenges, increase efficiency, and scale your startup to new heights. Choose wisely, and invest in tools that will not only meet your needs today but also grow with you as your business expands.

Building an Online Presence: Website, Social Media, and SEO

In today's digital age, establishing a strong online presence is more important than ever for businesses of all sizes. Whether you're a budding startup or a well-established company, your online visibility determines how easily potential customers can find you, engage with your brand, and ultimately make a purchase. Building an online presence is not just about having a website or posting on social media—it's about creating a cohesive, engaging, and accessible brand experience that resonates with your audience. In this chapter, we'll explore how to build an effective online presence through your website, social media, and SEO (search engine optimization).

1. The Foundation: Creating a Website That Works for You

Your website is often the first point of contact between your business and potential customers. It acts as your digital storefront, and a well-designed website can make a powerful impression. To start, your website needs to be professional, user-friendly, and optimized for conversions.

Design and User Experience: The design of your website should reflect your brand's personality and be visually appealing. But beyond aesthetics, the user experience (UX) is paramount. Ensure that your site is easy to navigate, loads quickly, and is responsive across all devices, from desktop computers to smartphones. A clean layout with intuitive navigation helps visitors find what they need without frustration.

Clear Call to Action (CTA): Every page on your website should have a clear call to action (CTA) that encourages visitors to take the next step, whether it's subscribing to a newsletter, making a purchase, or contacting you for more information. Your CTA should be prominent, easy to understand, and compelling enough to prompt immediate action.

Content and Trust Signals: Your website's content should be informative, helpful, and engaging. This includes high-quality copywriting, images, and videos that explain your products or services and how they benefit your audience. Additionally, trust signals such as customer testimonials, reviews, and case studies can reassure visitors that your business is reliable and credible.

Integrating E-Commerce (if applicable): If you're selling products, ensure that your website has an integrated e-commerce platform. A smooth, secure shopping experience that includes easy navigation, clear product descriptions, and multiple payment options is key to converting visitors into paying customers.

With a professional, easy-to-use website, you'll lay the groundwork for building your online presence and capturing the attention of potential customers.

2. Social Media: Engaging with Your Audience

Once your website is up and running, it's time to turn to social media. Social media platforms like Facebook, Instagram, Twitter, LinkedIn, and

TikTok allow businesses to connect with their audience in real-time, build relationships, and engage with followers on a personal level. But with so many platforms available, how do you choose the right ones?

Identify the Right Platforms for Your Business: Not every social media platform will be suitable for your business. If you're a B2B company, LinkedIn might be the best choice for professional networking, while visual-driven businesses like fashion, food, or travel may find a more engaging audience on Instagram. Facebook is still a dominant platform for reaching a broad demographic, while Twitter can be useful for real-time conversations and industry updates.

Create Consistent, Valuable Content: Social media is all about providing value to your audience. Share a mix of content, from educational posts and industry insights to behind-the-scenes glimpses of your business. High-quality images, videos, and infographics can capture attention and encourage followers to engage with your posts. Be consistent with your posting schedule so that your audience knows when to expect new content from you.

Engage with Your Followers: Social media is a two-way street. Don't just post and forget—actively engage with your followers by responding to comments, sharing user-generated content, and asking questions. Building a community around your brand creates trust and loyalty, which can lead to long-term customer relationships. If a follower tags your business in a post or leaves a positive comment, be sure to thank them, share their post, or offer incentives like discounts or giveaways.

Use Social Media Ads: Social media platforms offer highly targeted advertising options, allowing you to reach a specific audience based on location, interests, age, and more. Ads on platforms like Facebook and Instagram can be an effective way to increase your brand's visibility and drive traffic to your website.

By using social media to engage with your audience, you'll not only increase brand awareness but also create a loyal following that values your business.

3. SEO: Optimizing for Search Engines

Search engine optimization (SEO) is the art and science of optimizing your website and content to rank higher in search engine results pages (SERPs), like Google. When done correctly, SEO can drive organic traffic to your website and significantly increase your online visibility. Here's how to get started:

Keyword Research: The foundation of any successful SEO strategy is keyword research. Identify the terms and phrases that potential customers are searching for when looking for products or services like yours. Tools like Google Keyword Planner, SEMrush, and Ahrefs can help you discover keywords with high search volume and low competition. Once you have your list of target keywords, incorporate them naturally into your website's content, including headings, page titles, and meta descriptions.

Optimize On-Page SEO: On-page SEO refers to optimizing individual pages on your website for search engines. This includes using relevant keywords in your page titles, headers, image alt text, and URLs. Be sure to write compelling meta descriptions that summarize the page's content, as this is what appears in search results. Internal linking to other pages on your site also improves your SEO by making it easier for search engines to crawl your website.

Create High-Quality Content: Content is king when it comes to SEO. Google and other search engines prioritize websites that offer valuable, informative content. Regularly publish blog posts, articles, case studies, and other types of content that address your audience's pain points or questions. The more high-quality content you produce, the more likely it is that search engines will rank your website higher.

Mobile Optimization: With the increasing use of smartphones and tablets, it's essential that your website is mobile-friendly. Google uses mobile-first indexing, meaning it prioritizes mobile-optimized websites in search results. Make sure your website is responsive, meaning it automatically adjusts to fit various screen sizes, so visitors have a smooth experience regardless of the device they're using.

Build Backlinks: Backlinks—links from other reputable websites to your own—are an important ranking factor in SEO. Focus on building relationships with influencers, bloggers, and industry experts who can link to your content. High-quality backlinks not only boost your SEO but also enhance your credibility and authority in your industry.

Local SEO: If your business has a physical location or serves a specific geographic area, local SEO is essential. Set up and optimize your Google My Business profile, ensuring that your business information is accurate and up to date. Encourage customers to leave reviews, as positive reviews can boost your local rankings and attract more customers to your store.

4. Integrating Your Online Presence for Maximum Impact

Building a strong online presence is not just about having a website, being active on social media, and optimizing for SEO in isolation. For maximum impact, these elements must work together seamlessly. For example, your social media posts should link back to your website, where visitors can learn more about your products or services. Similarly, the content on your website should be optimized for SEO, helping search engines find and rank it.

Additionally, ensure that your branding is consistent across all online platforms. From your website design and logo to your social media profiles and messaging, maintain a unified brand identity that helps your audience recognize and trust your business.

Conclusion: Be Seen, Be Heard, and Be Found

Building an online presence takes time, effort, and consistency, but the results are well worth it. Your website serves as the foundation of your online presence, while social media allows you to engage with your audience on a deeper level. SEO ties everything together by ensuring that people can find you when they search for products or services like yours. By integrating these elements and remaining consistent in your efforts, you'll increase your brand visibility, build stronger relationships with your audience, and drive sustainable business growth.

Leveraging Automation and Analytics for Efficiency

In the world of startups, every decision counts, and time is one of your most valuable resources. As an entrepreneur, you're likely juggling multiple tasks at once, from customer service to marketing to financial planning. This is where automation and analytics can come to your rescue. By leveraging these powerful tools, you can streamline processes, improve decision-making, and ultimately free up time to focus on what really matters—growing your business.

1. The Power of Automation: Working Smarter, Not Harder

Automation refers to the use of technology to perform repetitive tasks without human intervention. By automating certain aspects of your business, you can save time, reduce errors, and ensure consistency. In the early stages of a startup, where resources are often limited, automation is a game-changer.

Email Marketing Automation: One of the most common and effective uses of automation is in email marketing. Platforms like Mailchimp and HubSpot allow you to automate email campaigns, so you don't have to send emails manually to each customer. You can set up automated workflows to send welcome emails, birthday discounts, or abandoned cart reminders without lifting a finger. Automation helps you stay connected with customers at the right time, increasing engagement and conversions without adding extra work.

Social Media Scheduling: Social media management can be time-consuming, especially when you're trying to stay active on multiple platforms. Tools like Buffer, Hootsuite, and Later allow you to schedule posts in advance, so you don't have to worry about posting in real-time. You can plan a week or even a month's worth of content in one sitting and let the automation tools handle the rest. This gives you more time to engage with your audience, create new content, or work on other important tasks.

Customer Support Automation: Customer support is essential for building a loyal client base, but it can become overwhelming as your business grows. Tools like Zendesk and Intercom offer automated responses to common customer inquiries, allowing you to resolve issues quickly without having to answer each question individually. Additionally, chatbots can be integrated into your website to handle basic customer queries, freeing up your team to focus on more complex issues.

Sales and Lead Management: Managing leads and sales processes can also benefit from automation. CRM tools like Salesforce and Pipedrive can help you automatically capture leads, send follow-up emails, and track sales opportunities. With automated workflows, you can move leads through the sales funnel without missing a beat. This ensures that no potential client slips through the cracks, and you're consistently nurturing relationships with minimal effort.

Automation not only makes your processes more efficient but also improves the customer experience. When tasks are automated, they're completed faster and with fewer mistakes, which results in more satisfied customers and a smoother-running business.

2. Analytics: Data-Driven Decisions for Smarter Growth

While automation helps you do more in less time, analytics provides the insights you need to make smarter, data-driven decisions. By understanding your business data, you can identify trends, spot opportunities, and fine-tune your strategies to maximize growth.

Website Analytics: Tools like Google Analytics are essential for understanding how visitors interact with your website. By tracking metrics such as page views, bounce rates, and conversion rates, you can identify areas for improvement. For example, if you notice a high bounce rate on a particular page, it could signal that the content is not engaging enough or the page isn't user-friendly. With these insights, you can optimize your site to improve user experience and increase conversions.

Social Media Analytics: Social media platforms like Instagram, Facebook, and Twitter offer built-in analytics tools that provide detailed insights into how your posts are performing. You can track metrics such as engagement rates, reach, and follower growth. This data allows you to see which content resonates most with your audience, enabling you to tailor future posts for maximum engagement. By understanding what works, you can refine your social media strategy and drive better results without wasting time on ineffective content.

Customer Analytics: Understanding your customers' behavior and preferences is key to providing a personalized experience. Tools like Google Analytics, Mixpanel, and Kissmetrics allow you to track customer behavior across various touchpoints, from website visits to purchases. You can segment your customers based on demographics, purchase history, and interests, which enables you to create targeted marketing campaigns and product recommendations. The more you understand your customers, the better you can serve them—and the higher your chances of converting them into repeat buyers.

Sales Analytics: Tracking sales performance is critical for understanding the health of your business. Tools like HubSpot Sales, Zoho CRM, and Freshsales can give you real-time insights into your sales pipeline, conversion rates, and revenue. You can track the performance of individual sales reps, identify bottlenecks in the sales process, and make adjustments to improve results. By analyzing sales data, you can identify which products or services are performing well, and which ones need more attention, allowing you to focus your efforts where they matter most.

Analytics can also help you understand the ROI of your marketing efforts. By tracking key performance indicators (KPIs), such as customer acquisition costs, customer lifetime value, and conversion rates, you can gauge the effectiveness of your campaigns and make adjustments to ensure you're spending your marketing budget wisely.

3. Integrating Automation and Analytics: The Ultimate Efficiency Boost

While both automation and analytics are powerful tools individually, the real magic happens when you integrate them. By combining automation with data-driven insights, you can optimize your operations and make smarter, faster decisions.

For example, let's say you're running an email marketing campaign. Using analytics, you can determine which subject lines, offers, or content types perform best with your audience. Once you have that data, you can set up automated workflows that incorporate these insights, ensuring that each email you send has the best chance of converting. Automation takes the manual work out of executing these campaigns, while analytics ensures you're always optimizing for the best possible results.

Similarly, if you're using a CRM to manage your leads, you can use analytics to track how they're moving through the sales funnel. If you notice that leads are getting stuck at a particular stage, you can set up automation to send timely follow-up emails or trigger additional actions to push them forward.

The integration of these two tools allows you to not only work more efficiently but also continuously improve your processes and outcomes. The data you collect through analytics informs the automation workflows you set up, creating a feedback loop that leads to better decision-making and business performance over time.

4. Scaling Your Business with Automation and Analytics

As your business grows, managing all aspects manually becomes increasingly difficult. Automation and analytics provide the scalability needed to handle larger volumes of customers, sales, and data. By setting up automated systems, you can maintain a high level of service without hiring additional staff. Meanwhile, analytics ensures that you're always making data-driven decisions, allowing you to scale your operations intelligently.

For example, automated customer service systems, like chatbots, can handle an influx of customer inquiries without overwhelming your support team. Meanwhile, analytics can help you identify which products are in high demand, so you can focus on scaling those aspects of your business first.

Conclusion: A Smarter, More Efficient Startup

In the fast-paced world of startups, efficiency is everything. Automation and analytics give you the power to work smarter, not harder. By automating repetitive tasks, you free up valuable time to focus on growing your business and engaging with your customers. And by leveraging analytics, you make informed, data-driven decisions that propel your business forward.

Together, these tools allow you to streamline your processes, improve customer experiences, and maximize your resources, ultimately setting your startup on a path to sustainable growth. So, embrace automation and analytics, and watch as they transform your business into a well-oiled machine ready to take on the world.

Chapter 7:

Navigating Challenges: Staying Resilient and Adaptable

Embarking on the entrepreneurial journey is like setting sail into uncharted waters. While the excitement of starting something new can be overwhelming, there's a reality that every business owner faces sooner or later—challenges. These challenges may come in the form of financial difficulties, market competition, or unexpected setbacks, and they often arrive at the most inconvenient times. But what distinguishes successful entrepreneurs is not the absence of obstacles, but their ability to stay resilient and adaptable when things get tough.

Resilience is the ability to bounce back from adversity, and adaptability is the skill to adjust your strategies in response to changing circumstances. Together, these qualities form the foundation for long-term success in business. In this chapter, we'll explore how to embrace setbacks as learning opportunities, stay flexible in the face of uncertainty, and keep moving forward no matter what obstacles come your way.

1. Embracing Failure as a Stepping Stone

Failure is a word that most entrepreneurs dread. But the truth is, every entrepreneur has faced failure at some point in their journey. It could be the failure of a product that didn't meet market expectations, a marketing campaign that didn't generate leads, or a partnership that didn't pan out. Instead of allowing these failures to define you, view them as stepping stones toward success.

One of the keys to resilience is embracing failure with a growth mindset. Failure is not a reflection of your worth or abilities, but rather a learning opportunity. Take the time to analyze what went wrong, extract valuable lessons, and move forward with a renewed sense of purpose. For example, if a product launch fails, ask yourself: What was the gap in the market? Why didn't customers respond the way you expected? What can you improve next time?

Resilient entrepreneurs don't let failures set them back for too long. They use setbacks to build a more solid foundation for future endeavors. Remember, every failure teaches you something new that can help you avoid the same mistakes in the future.

2. The Art of Adaptability: Adjusting to Change

In the fast-paced world of business, change is the only constant. Consumer preferences evolve, technology advances, and market dynamics shift. As an entrepreneur, your ability to adapt to these changes is critical for staying relevant and competitive.

Being adaptable doesn't mean constantly chasing new trends or jumping on every bandwagon. It's about being open-minded, flexible, and ready to adjust your business strategies when the situation demands it. For example, if a certain marketing tactic stops working, don't keep pushing the same strategy hoping it will suddenly deliver results. Instead, pivot your approach based on data and insights. The ability to quickly change direction when necessary can be the difference between success and failure.

Adapting doesn't only apply to marketing or products; it's also about being open to changes in your internal processes. Whether it's adopting new software for project management, revising team workflows, or redefining your business goals, adaptability helps you stay nimble and responsive.

3. Overcoming Financial Challenges

One of the most common challenges faced by entrepreneurs is managing finances, particularly in the early stages of a business. Cash flow problems, unexpected expenses, and difficulty securing funding can put a serious strain on your operations. However, overcoming these challenges requires a proactive mindset and strategic planning.

Financial resilience comes from understanding your cash flow, setting aside reserves for rainy days, and finding creative solutions when money gets tight. If you face a sudden downturn in revenue, consider rethinking your cost structure. Can you reduce unnecessary expenses? Are there opportunities to increase revenue through additional sales channels? When looking for funding, think outside the box. Crowdfunding, angel investors, and small business loans are all viable options beyond traditional bank loans.

Don't be afraid to seek professional advice from accountants or financial experts. They can help you navigate financial pitfalls, optimize your business model, and plan for the future. Building financial resilience means preparing for the unexpected and being willing to make tough decisions to ensure your business can weather any storm.

4. Managing Stress and Avoiding Burnout

The pressures of entrepreneurship can often lead to stress and burnout, particularly when challenges seem unrelenting. The key to maintaining resilience is not just about powering through the hardships but also about taking care of your mental and physical well-being. Stress and burnout can cloud your judgment, decrease productivity, and ultimately affect the long-term success of your business.

Managing stress involves setting clear boundaries, taking regular breaks, and practicing mindfulness or relaxation techniques. Whether it's going for a walk, meditating, or simply spending time with loved ones, make sure to recharge regularly. Additionally, delegating tasks and seeking support from your team can alleviate some of the pressure. A resilient entrepreneur knows when to step back, take a breather, and come back to work with a clear mind.

Another way to manage stress is by celebrating small wins. Every milestone, no matter how small, is a reminder of progress. Whether it's securing your first client or launching a successful ad campaign, acknowledging these victories can help lift your spirits and keep you motivated when the road gets tough.

5. Building a Support System

No entrepreneur is an island. As you navigate the ups and downs of building your business, it's essential to have a strong support system. This includes mentors, peers, friends, and family members who can offer advice, encouragement, and a fresh perspective when things feel overwhelming.

Mentorship is particularly valuable when facing challenges. A mentor is someone who has been through similar struggles and can offer guidance on how to overcome them. They can help you make tough decisions, avoid common mistakes, and keep you focused on your goals. Surrounding yourself with people who believe in you and your vision provides a sense of security and motivation to keep going.

Networking with fellow entrepreneurs also provides a wealth of insight. Join industry groups, attend networking events, or participate in online communities to connect with others who are navigating the same challenges. The support and advice you gain from these connections can help you stay resilient and motivated.

6. Staying Focused on Long-Term Goals

While challenges may arise in the short term, it's important to maintain focus on your long-term vision. Entrepreneurship is a marathon, not a sprint, and it's easy to get bogged down by immediate obstacles. However, resilient entrepreneurs keep their eyes on the bigger picture.

When setbacks occur, revisit your mission and vision. Remind yourself why you started the business in the first place. This helps put challenges into perspective and gives you the motivation to keep pushing forward. Break down your long-term goals into smaller, manageable tasks, and celebrate each small win along the way. This creates a sense of momentum, which can help you power through difficult times.

7. Conclusion: Growing Stronger Through Adversity

Navigating challenges is an inherent part of the entrepreneurial journey. The key to success lies not in avoiding challenges, but in how you respond to them. By cultivating resilience, staying adaptable, managing stress, and building a strong support system, you can turn obstacles into opportunities for growth.

The road to entrepreneurship is rarely smooth, but with the right mindset and strategies, you can overcome any challenge that comes your way. Keep pushing forward, stay flexible, and embrace the lessons that come from adversity. In the end, it's not the challenges you face, but how you handle them, that will determine your success as an entrepreneur.

Common Hurdles for New Entrepreneurs

Starting a business is a thrilling venture, filled with excitement and a sense of possibility. However, the road to entrepreneurial success is often paved with obstacles. Whether you're launching a small local business or a tech startup, the challenges you face early on can feel overwhelming. While every entrepreneur's journey is unique, there are common hurdles that nearly all new business owners encounter. The key to navigating these challenges is understanding them ahead of time and developing strategies to overcome them.

1. Financial Challenges

One of the most significant hurdles for new entrepreneurs is managing finances. Many business owners struggle with securing adequate funding, balancing cash flow, and managing expenses. Starting a business requires initial investment, but accessing that capital can be tricky. Small businesses often rely on personal savings, loans, or outside investors to get started, but even after the initial funding is in place, cash flow remains a constant concern. Poor cash flow management can be the downfall of many new ventures, as it affects the ability to pay bills, employees, and invest in growth.

To address financial hurdles, new entrepreneurs must create a solid financial plan, track expenses carefully, and ensure they have a cushion for unexpected costs. Seeking professional help from accountants or financial advisors can also help avoid common pitfalls, especially when it comes to tax obligations and long-term planning.

2. Time Management Struggles

In the early stages of a business, entrepreneurs often wear many hats. From product development to marketing to customer service, it can feel like there are endless tasks that demand your attention. Time management becomes a critical skill to master, as it's easy to get overwhelmed with too many responsibilities. Often, new entrepreneurs spend long hours working in their business, leaving little time for strategic thinking or self-care.

To overcome time management challenges, entrepreneurs should prioritize their tasks, delegate responsibilities when possible, and set clear goals. It's also important to recognize when to step away and recharge, as burnout can quickly reduce productivity and creativity. Using tools like time-tracking apps and project management software can also streamline processes and help you stay focused on what matters most.

3. Building a Customer Base

Acquiring customers is another significant hurdle for new businesses. No matter how great your product or service is, if you don't have customers, your business will not survive. The challenge lies not only in finding customers but also in retaining them. Many new businesses struggle with customer acquisition due to lack of brand recognition, ineffective marketing strategies, or simply not understanding their target market.

To overcome this challenge, entrepreneurs must invest time in understanding their target audience, identifying their needs, and tailoring their marketing efforts accordingly. Conducting market research, engaging with customers through surveys, and analyzing competitor strategies can help you create a solid plan to build and grow your customer base. Building relationships with your customers through excellent service and communication is equally important for retention.

4. Marketing and Branding

Marketing and branding are crucial to the success of any business, but for new entrepreneurs, they can be particularly challenging. You may have a fantastic product, but if you don't know how to effectively promote it, your business will struggle. Marketing can be overwhelming because there are so many strategies and channels available, from social media advertising to search engine optimization (SEO) to influencer partnerships.

With so many options, it's easy to feel lost or unsure where to start.

New entrepreneurs often make the mistake of trying to do everything at once, spreading their efforts too thin across multiple platforms. Instead, it's better to focus on a few key channels that are most likely to reach your target audience. Building a strong brand identity that resonates with customers is also essential for standing out in a competitive market. Consistency in messaging, visual design, and tone will help build recognition and trust.

5. Legal and Compliance Issues

Navigating legal requirements can be a daunting task for new entrepreneurs. There are various legal hurdles to consider when starting a business, from registering the company to understanding tax obligations, and protecting intellectual property. Compliance with industry regulations is another critical area, especially in sectors like healthcare, finance, and tech. Many new business owners underestimate the importance of legal matters and neglect to take the necessary steps to protect their business.

To avoid legal issues, it's important to research the legal requirements in your industry and consult with legal professionals. Whether it's drafting contracts, applying for licenses, or setting up trademarks, taking the time to ensure your business is legally sound can prevent costly mistakes down the road.

6. Scaling the Business

Once your business is off the ground, the next challenge is figuring out how to scale it. Scaling requires a different set of skills, including managing increased demand, hiring more staff, and expanding your operations. For many new entrepreneurs, scaling can be a double-edged sword. On the one hand, growth is exciting; on the other hand, it requires significant investment of time, energy, and money.

Scaling is often a delicate balance. You need to ensure that your systems, processes, and infrastructure can handle increased operations. This means having the right team in place, automating tasks when possible, and carefully managing finances to avoid overstretching resources. New entrepreneurs should also understand that growth takes time and effort—scaling too quickly without proper planning can lead to significant setbacks.

7. Competition and Market Saturation

No matter the industry, new businesses face the challenge of competition. Whether you're in a crowded marketplace or entering an emerging industry, competitors are likely to be a constant factor. Many new entrepreneurs struggle with how to differentiate themselves from the competition, especially when they don't yet have the brand recognition or resources to stand out.

To navigate this challenge, new business owners must focus on finding their unique selling proposition (USP). What makes your business different from others in your industry? Is it your pricing, quality, customer service, or innovation? Identifying and communicating your USP clearly will help you carve out a niche and attract customers who value what you offer.

8. Lack of Experience

Perhaps the most common challenge for new entrepreneurs is a lack of experience. Starting a business from scratch requires a wide range of skills, including management, sales, marketing, and finance. Many entrepreneurs enter the world of business with little prior experience, and this inexperience can lead to costly mistakes.

Fortunately, this hurdle can be overcome with continuous learning, seeking mentorship, and leveraging resources such as online courses, workshops, and networking events. Surrounding yourself with experts or building a team that complements your skill set can also help bridge the experience gap. Recognize that you don't have to know everything, but you do need to be proactive in learning and growing along the way.

9. Self-Doubt and Mental Health

Entrepreneurship is an emotional rollercoaster. From moments of triumph to periods of doubt and uncertainty, the mental and emotional toll can be intense. Self-doubt is a natural part of the entrepreneurial experience, but it can also paralyze decision-making and hinder progress. The pressure to succeed, coupled with the isolation that many entrepreneurs feel, can also lead to burnout, anxiety, and even depression.

To tackle this challenge, entrepreneurs must prioritize mental health. Building a support system of family, friends, mentors, and fellow business owners can provide much-needed encouragement and advice. Taking regular breaks, practicing mindfulness, and celebrating small wins are all important ways to combat burnout and stay motivated.

Conclusion

Entrepreneurship is an exciting journey filled with potential, but it's also one that comes with its fair share of challenges. The good news is that with the right mindset, strategic planning, and a willingness to learn, these hurdles are not insurmountable. By understanding the common obstacles that new entrepreneurs face, you'll be better prepared to handle them and move your business forward. Every challenge is an opportunity to learn, grow, and ultimately succeed. Stay resilient, keep learning, and never forget that every great entrepreneur started out just like you—with a dream and the determination to turn it into reality.

Problem-Solving and Decision-Making Frameworks: Navigating Challenges with Confidence

As an entrepreneur, the ability to solve problems and make decisions effectively is one of the most essential skills you can possess. Every day brings new challenges, and the way you approach them can have a significant impact on your business's success. Whether you're deciding which product to launch next, how to handle a customer complaint, or how to adjust your business strategy in response to market changes, the decision-making process can make or break your venture.

Fortunately, there are proven problem-solving and decision-making frameworks that can help guide your thought process, reduce uncertainty, and increase your chances of making well-informed, confident decisions. In this chapter, we'll explore some of the most effective frameworks that can be used by entrepreneurs to tackle challenges head-on and navigate the complexities of running a business.

1. The SWOT Analysis: Understanding Your Strengths, Weaknesses, Opportunities, and Threats

One of the simplest yet most powerful tools for decision-making is the SWOT analysis. SWOT stands for Strengths, Weaknesses, Opportunities, and Threats, and this framework provides a clear snapshot of your business's current position. The purpose of a SWOT analysis is to help you understand both the internal and external factors that could influence your decisions.

Start by identifying your business's strengths—what do you excel at? Do you have a unique product, a loyal customer base, or a strong brand reputation? Next, acknowledge your weaknesses. Are there areas where your business could improve, such as customer service, operational efficiency, or marketing efforts? Once you've done that, focus on the opportunities available in the market. Are there emerging trends, new technologies, or untapped markets you can capitalize on? Finally, consider the threats you face. These could be from competitors, regulatory changes, or market shifts that may negatively impact your business.

By using the SWOT analysis, you can make informed decisions by leveraging your strengths, addressing your weaknesses, seizing opportunities, and mitigating threats. It's a comprehensive framework that can help you evaluate all aspects of a problem and guide you toward the best solution.

2. The 5 Whys: Digging Deeper into Problems

When you encounter a problem, it's tempting to address the symptoms rather than the root cause. However, surface-level solutions rarely lead to lasting success. This is where the 5 Whys technique comes in. Developed by Toyota as part of its Lean Manufacturing process, the 5 Whys is a simple yet powerful tool for identifying the root cause of a problem.

The process involves asking "why" five times to drill deeper into the problem. For example, let's say sales have been declining. The first "Why" might be, "Why are sales down?" The answer could be "Customers aren't engaging with our marketing campaigns." The next "Why" could be, "Why aren't customers engaging with our campaigns?" The answer might be "The messaging is unclear and doesn't resonate with their needs." You continue asking "why" until you've identified the core issue.

By applying the 5 Whys, you can avoid wasting time and resources on short-term fixes. Instead, you get to the heart of the problem, which allows you to develop more effective, long-term solutions. The 5 Whys is an excellent tool when you need to break down a complex issue and uncover hidden causes.

3. The Eisenhower Matrix: Prioritizing Tasks and Decisions

In a busy business environment, it's easy to become overwhelmed with the sheer volume of decisions that need to be made. Whether it's deciding which customer complaints to address first or which projects to prioritize, staying organized is key to making efficient decisions. The Eisenhower Matrix is a tool that helps you prioritize tasks by urgency and importance, ensuring that you focus on what truly matters.

The Eisenhower Matrix is divided into four quadrants:

Urgent and Important: Tasks that require immediate attention and have a significant impact on your business. These should be your top priority.

Important but Not Urgent: Tasks that are essential for long-term success but don't require immediate action. These are the activities that you should schedule and work on regularly.

Urgent but Not Important: Tasks that demand your attention but don't have a major impact on your goals. These can often be delegated to others.

Neither Urgent nor Important: Tasks that don't contribute to your business's goals and should be minimized or eliminated.

By using the Eisenhower Matrix, you can make decisions with clarity and avoid spending time on tasks that won't help you achieve your bigger objectives. It helps you stay focused on what truly moves the needle for your business.

4. The Cost-Benefit Analysis: Weighing Your Options

When faced with multiple choices, the cost-benefit analysis can help you make an informed decision by comparing the potential costs and benefits of each option. This decision-making framework involves outlining the pros and cons of a particular course of action, as well as estimating the financial, time, and resource investments required.

For example, if you're deciding whether to invest in a new marketing campaign, you would list all the costs associated with it—such as advertising expenses, design costs, and time commitments. Then, you would compare these costs to the potential benefits, like increased brand awareness, higher sales, or greater customer engagement. If the benefits outweigh the costs, the decision becomes easier. If not, it might be worth reconsidering or exploring alternative options.

A cost-benefit analysis is particularly useful when you're making decisions that involve significant investments of time, money, or resources. It helps you evaluate whether the rewards justify the risks, ensuring that you make choices that are financially sound and strategically aligned with your business goals.

5. The Decision Matrix: Evaluating Multiple Options

When you're faced with multiple alternatives, it can be hard to determine which one is the best. The decision matrix (also called the prioritization matrix) is a framework that helps you objectively evaluate different options based on specific criteria. This is especially useful when you have to choose between several good ideas or strategies.

To use the decision matrix, create a table with each option as a row and the criteria for evaluation as columns. Then, score each option on a scale (for example, 1 to 5) based on how well it meets each criterion. Multiply the scores by the weight of each criterion (if some factors are more important than others) and sum the totals. The option with the highest score is usually the most favorable choice.

For example, if you're choosing between three potential suppliers, you might evaluate them based on criteria like price, quality, customer service, and delivery times. By scoring each supplier and adding up the totals, you can make a more objective and data-driven decision.

6. The OODA Loop: Responding Quickly and Effectively

In the fast-paced world of entrepreneurship, decisions often need to be made quickly. The OODA loop (Observe, Orient, Decide, Act) is a framework that helps you make rapid decisions in high-pressure situations. Originally developed for military strategy, the OODA loop can be applied to business to help entrepreneurs respond to changing circumstances and unexpected challenges.

The process begins with observing the situation and gathering relevant information. Next, you orient yourself by analyzing the data and considering your options. Then, you decide on the best course of action, and finally, you act by implementing the decision. Once you've acted, you observe the results and repeat the loop, making adjustments as needed.

The OODA loop is particularly useful in situations where speed is essential, and you need to make decisions on the fly. It encourages quick thinking, continuous learning, and adaptability.

Conclusion: Developing Your Decision-Making Muscles

Problem-solving and decision-making are skills that improve with practice. By applying these frameworks, you can approach business challenges with a clear, methodical mindset and make more informed, confident decisions. Whether you're analyzing a problem with a SWOT analysis, prioritizing tasks with the Eisenhower Matrix, or evaluating options with a decision matrix, these tools help you cut through complexity and focus on what matters most.

As an entrepreneur, your ability to make smart, timely decisions can determine the future of your business. So, embrace these frameworks, learn from your experiences, and keep sharpening your decision-making muscles. With the right approach, you'll be able to navigate even the toughest challenges with ease and confidence.

Building a Support Network and Mentorship: Strength in Connection

As an entrepreneur, you're likely to face numerous challenges and moments of doubt along your journey. These can range from the day-to-day struggles of running a business to the larger existential questions about your vision and purpose. In these moments, having a support network and access to mentorship can make all the difference. Surrounding yourself with a group of trusted advisors, fellow entrepreneurs, and industry experts will not only help you tackle problems but also provide the emotional and professional support you need to push through tough times.

Building a solid support network and finding the right mentors are essential steps in growing your business and maintaining your mental and emotional well-being. These relationships provide you with guidance, advice, and encouragement—tools that are crucial for long-term success. Let's dive into why a support network and mentorship matter and how you can actively build both.

Why a Support Network Is Crucial for Entrepreneurs

Running a business is incredibly isolating. While you may have employees or partners, you might still find yourself facing difficult decisions alone. A support network fills this gap. It's a group of people—whether friends, family, peers, or professionals—who have your back when times get tough. These individuals provide the emotional backing you need to stay motivated and the practical advice that helps you make informed decisions.

At times, the pressure of entrepreneurship can feel overwhelming, and the weight of your responsibilities may feel like it's all on your shoulders. When you have a support network, you're not alone. These people can offer perspectives that you might not have considered, helping you break out of your own mental rut. A great support network will not only listen to your ideas but also provide constructive criticism and honest feedback. They'll push you to be better, hold you accountable, and celebrate your successes with you.

Moreover, your support network doesn't just give you emotional strength; it also provides invaluable resources. Through your connections, you may discover new business opportunities, potential collaborations, or introductions to other industry professionals. The people you surround yourself with can be a source of ideas and inspiration, opening doors to possibilities that you might have missed on your own.

The Power of Mentorship

While a support network is vital for emotional and practical support, mentorship takes this relationship to the next level by providing expert guidance. Mentors are typically individuals who have experience in the industry or field you're working in and have walked the path you're just beginning to take. A mentor acts as both a coach and a guide, sharing their knowledge and experiences to help you avoid common pitfalls and make smarter, more informed decisions.

Having a mentor means you have access to someone who has already navigated the complex waters of entrepreneurship. They can provide advice on scaling your business, handling challenges, and making tough decisions. More importantly, they can offer a unique perspective based on their own mistakes and successes. These lessons are invaluable as you chart your own course in the business world.

Mentors are also excellent sounding boards. They listen to your ideas without judgment and give you honest, unbiased feedback. This can be especially important when you're facing a critical decision or are unsure of the direction your business should take. A good mentor will help you think through your options, consider the long-term consequences, and offer insights based on their own experience.

Perhaps most importantly, mentors can help you build confidence. Starting a business can be an intimidating endeavor, and self-doubt is a common companion for many entrepreneurs. Having someone who believes in your potential and can remind you of your strengths when things get tough is incredibly powerful. Your mentor can be the voice of reason when you're ready to throw in the towel and the motivator when you feel like giving up.

How to Find and Build a Support Network

Now that we've established the importance of a support network and mentorship, let's look at how you can build one. The first step is to start by identifying the types of people who could be most helpful to you. A strong support network should consist of people from different backgrounds, perspectives, and areas of expertise. These might include:

Fellow Entrepreneurs: Other people in the same boat as you who understand the struggles of starting and running a business. They can offer support and share similar experiences.

Industry Experts: Professionals who have been in your industry for a long time and can provide insights into trends, challenges, and opportunities.

Family and Friends: People who care about you and can provide emotional support, even if they don't understand every aspect of your business.

Peers from Networking Events: People you meet at industry conferences, workshops, or networking events who may become long-term contacts.

Start by attending networking events, industry conferences, and workshops. These places are filled with like-minded individuals, and you'll have the chance to make connections that could evolve into lasting relationships. Online communities and social media platforms like LinkedIn, Twitter, and Facebook groups also provide opportunities to connect with other entrepreneurs, business owners, and professionals.

Once you've identified the individuals who could become part of your support network, build meaningful, authentic relationships with them. Engage in conversations, be open about your challenges, and take the time to listen to others. Offer help and support where you can—it's a two-way street. The more you invest in these relationships, the more you'll gain from them.

How to Find and Approach Mentors

Mentorship is often a more formal relationship than a support network. Finding the right mentor involves more than simply asking someone for advice. It's about building a connection based on trust, respect, and a shared vision for your success. Here's how to approach finding and cultivating a mentor-mentee relationship:

1. Identify Your Needs: Before seeking a mentor, take time to reflect on what areas of your business or personal development you want help with. Do you need guidance on marketing, scaling, leadership, or financial management? Knowing what you want from a mentor will help you find the right fit.

2. Look for Relevant Experience: A mentor should have experience in the areas where you need support. Look for individuals who have already navigated the challenges you face and who have the skills and knowledge to guide you. Industry leaders, successful entrepreneurs, or experienced professionals are often great choices.

3. Reach Out with Specific Requests: When approaching a potential mentor, be specific about why you admire their work and what you hope to learn from them. Make sure to express your respect for their time, and show that you're committed to learning. People are more likely to agree to mentor someone who demonstrates initiative and respect for their expertise.

4. Be Open to Feedback: Mentorship is about learning and growing, and that means being open to constructive criticism. A good mentor will challenge you and push you to do better, so be prepared to receive feedback, even if it's difficult to hear.

5. Offer Value in Return: While mentorship is often a one-sided relationship in terms of guidance, it's still important to think about ways you can give back to your mentor. Whether it's offering to assist them with a project or simply sharing your progress, showing gratitude and offering value can help solidify the relationship.

The Long-Term Benefits of a Support Network and Mentorship

Building a strong support network and cultivating meaningful mentor relationships takes time, but the rewards are immense. These connections provide you with a safety net of advice, encouragement, and opportunities that will help you grow your business more effectively and sustainably.

Having people who believe in you, understand your challenges, and offer valuable insights can increase your resilience and boost your chances of success. Whether you need emotional support during tough times, professional advice on a difficult decision, or the motivation to keep going, your support network and mentors are there to guide you.

Ultimately, the path to entrepreneurial success is rarely walked alone. By surrounding yourself with the right people and tapping into the wisdom of those who have already navigated the road, you'll have the confidence and resources to face whatever challenges lie ahead.

Chapter 8:

Scaling Your Business: Strategies for Sustainable Growth

Growing a business is one of the most exciting yet challenging aspects of entrepreneurship. In the early days, you hustle to get your product or service off the ground, managing everything from sales to customer service. But once your business gains traction, the next hurdle is scaling — expanding your operations in a way that continues to deliver value while maintaining quality and efficiency. The key to sustainable growth lies in a careful balance between expanding your capacity and preserving the essence of what made your business successful in the first place.

Scaling is not about simply increasing the number of customers or sales. It's about positioning your business to handle growth smoothly, without overstretching your resources or sacrificing quality.

In this chapter, we will explore key strategies to scale your business sustainably and ensure that the growth you experience is both profitable and long-lasting.

1. Streamline Your Operations

Before you can think about growing your business, it's essential to optimize your current operations. If your processes are inefficient or your systems are not scalable, then adding more customers or increasing production could lead to chaos, errors, or missed opportunities. The first step in scaling is ensuring that your operations are streamlined and capable of handling an increase in demand.

Start by identifying bottlenecks or inefficiencies in your workflow. Are there manual tasks that could be automated? Are there redundancies in your processes? A thorough evaluation of your business processes will highlight areas for improvement. Consider investing in software tools that can automate administrative tasks like accounting, inventory management, or scheduling, freeing up time for more strategic activities. By making your operations more efficient, you can scale without increasing the risk of mistakes or delays.

Another key part of streamlining is improving your supply chain. A strong, reliable supply chain is critical to meeting the demands of a growing customer base. Work closely with your suppliers and partners to ensure that they can handle the increased volume as your business grows. Building these relationships now will pay off when you need them most.

2. Focus on Customer Retention

While acquiring new customers is vital for growth, it's equally important to focus on retaining the customers you already have. In fact, increasing customer retention by just 5% can lead to a significant boost in profits. Loyal customers not only buy from you repeatedly, but they also refer others, reducing your cost of acquisition.

To retain customers, make sure your products or services continue to meet or exceed their expectations. Quality control becomes even more important as you scale, and it's essential to stay true to the values and promises you made to your customers in the early days. Offer excellent customer service and make it easy for customers to get in touch with you if they have concerns or feedback.

Loyalty programs, special offers, and personalized experiences can also go a long way in keeping customers happy. Use data to understand customer preferences and anticipate their needs. By showing customers that you care about their satisfaction, you create advocates who will help fuel your business's growth.

3. Expand Your Product or Service Offering

Diversifying your product or service offerings is a natural way to scale your business. By offering additional products or services that complement what you're already selling, you can tap into new revenue streams and meet the evolving needs of your existing customers. However, diversification should be done thoughtfully and in line with your core business values.

Before introducing new products or services, consider the following questions:

Does this expansion align with the needs of my target market?

Can I deliver this new offering with the same level of quality and customer service that has made my brand successful?

What are the financial and operational implications of this expansion?

If done correctly, expanding your product or service line can increase your market share, reduce your dependency on a single product or service, and create more opportunities for upselling. However, be careful not to stretch your resources too thin or lose focus on what made your original product or service unique.

4. Invest in Your Team

A growing business requires a team that can manage the increased workload and drive the company forward. As you scale, one of your most important tasks will be building a strong, reliable team. This means hiring the right people and investing in their development.

Start by identifying the key roles that need to be filled. Do you need more people in sales, marketing, customer service, or operations? Hiring strategically is essential—bringing in people who are not only skilled but also share your vision for the company.

Once you've hired the right team, invest in their growth. Offer training programs, mentorship, and opportunities for advancement. A motivated, well-trained team is more likely to perform well as the company expands, and their satisfaction will improve retention rates as well. Don't forget to foster a positive company culture that values collaboration, innovation, and transparency. A great team will be your most valuable asset as you scale.

5. Leverage Technology

As your business grows, it becomes increasingly difficult to manage everything manually. Technology is one of the most powerful tools you can use to scale. From project management tools to customer relationship management (CRM) software, there are countless technological solutions that can help you manage increased demand without sacrificing efficiency.

Investing in the right technology can improve everything from communication and project tracking to marketing and customer service. For example, automating repetitive tasks such as email marketing, inventory tracking, or payroll can free up your time to focus on strategic decisions. Cloud-based tools allow your team to collaborate seamlessly, regardless of location, making it easier to scale your operations without adding significant overhead.

Be sure to regularly evaluate your technological needs as your business grows. What tools will help you stay organized and streamline your operations? Stay ahead of the curve by adopting new technologies that can provide a competitive edge and increase your business's efficiency.

6. Secure Funding for Expansion

Scaling a business often requires an infusion of capital. Whether you're investing in new equipment, expanding your team, or increasing your marketing efforts, funding is essential to scale sustainably. There are various ways to secure funding, depending on the stage of your business and the amount of capital you need.

If you're just starting to scale, consider looking into small business loans, grants, or crowdfunding campaigns. These options can provide you with the capital you need without giving up equity in your business. As you continue to grow, you might consider seeking investment from venture capitalists or angel investors, especially if you're looking to make a significant leap in your growth trajectory.

When seeking funding, ensure that you have a solid business plan in place, complete with projections for future growth and a clear strategy for how the funds will be used. Investors and lenders want to know that you have a well-thought-out plan and are capable of using the funds efficiently.

7. Keep Your Financials in Check

Finally, as you scale, it's essential to keep a close eye on your finances. Growing your business means more revenue, but it also means increased expenses. Keeping track of cash flow, profit margins, and operational costs is critical to maintaining profitability as your business expands.

Hire a competent accountant or use financial management software to ensure that your business stays on top of its finances. Regularly reviewing your financial statements will help you make informed decisions and identify areas where you can cut costs or reinvest for future growth.

Conclusion

Scaling a business is not something that happens overnight. It requires careful planning, strategic decision-making, and a deep understanding of your market and operations. By streamlining your processes, focusing on customer retention, investing in your team, leveraging technology, securing funding, and keeping your financials in check, you can position your business for long-term success.

The key to sustainable growth is not just expanding for the sake of expansion, but doing so in a way that allows you to maintain the core values and quality that made your business successful in the first place. With the right strategies, you can scale your business in a way that is both profitable and sustainable, setting the stage for continued success for years to come.

Identifying Growth Opportunities

As an entrepreneur, one of the most exhilarating aspects of building your business is the constant search for growth opportunities. While the early stages of your business may focus primarily on establishing your brand and securing your first customers, once your business has gained some traction, identifying growth opportunities becomes the key to taking your business to the next level. This process involves more than just expanding your customer base; it requires a strategic approach to understanding market trends, exploring new markets, and leveraging existing resources in innovative ways.

But how exactly do you identify these growth opportunities? And how can you ensure that you're tapping into the right ones for long-term success? Let's dive into the strategies you can use to spot potential growth avenues for your business, whether you're scaling up, diversifying your offerings, or entering new markets.

1. Analyze Your Current Customer Base

Your existing customers are one of the richest sources of information when it comes to identifying growth opportunities. Understanding their needs, preferences, and pain points is not only crucial for improving your products and services, but it also opens doors to new ways to expand your offerings.

Take a deep dive into customer feedback—surveys, online reviews, and one-on-one conversations can give you a wealth of insight into what your customers value most and what they feel could be improved.

Once you have a clear picture of your current customer base, you can look for ways to enhance your offerings. Are there additional features or complementary products you can introduce? Maybe there are untapped markets within your current customer demographic that you can address with new services or products. For example, if you sell athletic wear, expanding into accessories like gym bags or yoga mats could be a natural next step. By serving your existing customers better and giving them more options, you can drive loyalty and boost sales.

2. Keep an Eye on Market Trends

Markets evolve, and so do consumer preferences. To stay ahead of the curve, it's essential to keep a pulse on market trends. Pay attention to shifts in consumer behavior, technological advancements, regulatory changes, and competitor actions. For instance, if you notice that eco-conscious products are gaining popularity, you may want to consider incorporating sustainable practices into your offerings. Similarly, trends such as remote work and the digital transformation of industries could present opportunities for tech-based services, such as offering virtual tools, remote team-building experiences, or online consulting.

Market research is invaluable when it comes to spotting new opportunities. Tools like Google Trends, industry reports, and social media can provide a wealth of real-time data about emerging trends and growing sectors. By identifying these trends early, you can position your business to take advantage of opportunities before they become mainstream. Whether it's offering an innovative product or targeting an underserved demographic, market trends provide insights into where demand is heading, giving you a competitive edge.

3. Diversify Your Product or Service Line

One of the most straightforward ways to drive growth is to diversify your product or service offerings. If your current offerings have found success, it might be time to expand them to appeal to a broader audience or address additional needs. Diversification doesn't always mean creating something entirely new—it could be as simple as modifying your existing products to cater to different customer segments or improving your service to make it more comprehensive.

Take the time to evaluate what your customers need that you aren't yet offering. Is there a gap in the market that aligns with your expertise? For example, if you own a coffee shop, adding new menu items or offering subscription services could attract new customers. Alternatively, you could consider moving into related areas, such as selling branded merchandise or offering coffee brewing equipment. The key is to stay true to your brand while exploring ways to enhance the value you provide to your customers.

4. Expand Into New Markets

Another effective way to identify growth opportunities is by expanding into new markets. This can mean targeting different geographic regions, catering to new customer segments, or introducing your products to international markets. Expanding into new markets is a powerful way to grow your customer base and increase revenue, but it also requires careful research and preparation.

Before entering a new market, it's critical to conduct thorough market research to understand the local demand, potential competitors, and cultural nuances that might impact your business. For example, if you plan to expand internationally, you'll need to understand local regulations, taxes, and consumer preferences. If you're targeting new demographics—such as a younger or older age group—you may need to adjust your messaging, pricing strategy, or even the features of your product to suit their needs.

In some cases, entering a new market might also mean leveraging partnerships with local businesses or influencers to create brand awareness. Collaborations can reduce the risks associated with entering an unfamiliar market while providing instant credibility and access to a wider audience.

5. Embrace Digital Transformation

Technology has revolutionized the way businesses operate, and embracing digital tools can open up a world of growth opportunities. From online marketing to e-commerce platforms, digital transformation can help you reach more customers, streamline operations, and enhance your customer experience.

If you're not already leveraging digital tools, now is the time to start. This might include launching an e-commerce site if you haven't already, using social media platforms to increase brand visibility, or adopting customer relationship management (CRM) systems to better manage customer interactions. Digital marketing channels like social media, email campaigns, and search engine optimization (SEO) offer cost-effective ways to reach your audience and attract new customers.

If your business already has an online presence, you might want to explore ways to expand it. Consider offering virtual events, online consultations, or subscription-based services that can appeal to customers who prefer digital solutions. Integrating digital tools into your business model can increase accessibility, enhance customer engagement, and help you tap into the growing trend of online commerce.

6. Leverage Strategic Partnerships

Partnerships can be a powerful vehicle for business growth. By collaborating with other companies, you can reach new customers, access new resources, and share costs. Look for potential partners whose products or services complement yours, and explore ways you can work together for mutual benefit.

For example, if you run a fitness equipment business, partnering with a health-focused brand or fitness influencer could be an excellent way to boost visibility and attract customers from their established audience. Similarly, collaborating with local businesses for joint promotions or co-branding opportunities can expose your brand to new customers. When done right, strategic partnerships can lead to increased credibility, wider exposure, and more sales.

7. Improve Customer Experience

Sometimes, the best growth opportunities lie not in finding new customers but in enhancing the experience of your existing ones. A positive customer experience can lead to repeat business, increased customer loyalty, and word-of-mouth referrals—all of which are critical for growth.

Start by evaluating every touchpoint in your customer journey. From the initial inquiry to post-purchase follow-up, how can you improve the overall experience? Maybe it's offering personalized recommendations, improving delivery times, or providing exceptional customer support. The more value you add at each stage of the customer journey, the more likely customers will return and recommend your business to others.

Another great opportunity for growth is implementing a referral program that rewards loyal customers for bringing in new clients. By incentivizing your existing customer base, you not only encourage loyalty but also harness the power of word-of-mouth marketing to attract new business.

Conclusion

Identifying growth opportunities is a dynamic and ongoing process. Whether through expanding your product offerings, entering new markets, or embracing digital tools, the key is to remain proactive and adaptable. Always be on the lookout for ways to improve, diversify, and innovate—because the next big opportunity might be just around the corner. By staying customer-focused, keeping up with market trends, and leveraging partnerships and technology, you'll be well on your way to scaling your business and achieving long-term success.

Hiring and Building a Team

As an entrepreneur, one of the most important steps you'll take in scaling your business is hiring the right team. While the journey to success often starts with you—your vision, your drive, and your ideas—no one can build a thriving business alone. As your company grows, the need for talented, motivated individuals who share your vision becomes more critical than ever. Building a strong, cohesive team is not just about filling roles; it's about finding the right people who will help propel your business forward.

Hiring the right team is both an art and a science. It's about aligning your company's goals with the strengths and potential of your team members. But where do you begin? What should you look for when hiring? How do you create a culture that attracts top talent? Let's explore how to hire and build a team that will help take your business to new heights.

1. Define Your Company's Needs

The first step in building a great team is understanding what your company truly needs.

This is more than just knowing that you need a marketing person or a financial expert; it's about understanding the unique skills and qualities that each role requires to thrive within your organization.

Start by identifying the key areas of your business that need support. Do you need someone to handle operations, marketing, or sales? Or perhaps you need someone with specialized skills, like a tech expert or a graphic designer. It's crucial to clearly define the responsibilities and expectations of each position you want to fill. This clarity will not only help you attract the right candidates but also set the stage for long-term success by ensuring that every team member is aligned with the company's objectives.

You should also consider the personality traits that would complement your company culture. For example, if your business thrives on collaboration and innovation, you might prioritize individuals who are team-oriented, creative, and flexible. On the other hand, if your company focuses on precision and quality control, a candidate with strong attention to detail and a methodical approach might be your best bet.

2. Attracting the Right Candidates

Once you've identified your hiring needs, the next step is attracting the right candidates. A compelling job listing is a great starting point, but it's also essential to market your company as a place people want to work. Talented individuals are often attracted to organizations that offer more than just a paycheck—they want to be part of a company with a clear mission, strong leadership, and opportunities for growth.

To attract the right candidates, be sure to showcase your company culture, values, and vision in your job postings and on your website. Transparency is key. Potential hires should understand what it's like to work for your company and what they can expect in terms of growth opportunities, work-life balance, and team dynamics.

Social media platforms like LinkedIn, Twitter, and even Instagram can also be powerful tools for attracting top talent. Share behind-the-scenes glimpses of your workplace, highlight team achievements, and post job openings to create awareness of your company's culture. Networking—whether through industry events, online communities, or word-of-mouth—can also play a significant role in finding qualified candidates.

Lastly, consider working with recruitment agencies or job boards that specialize in startup hiring. These resources can help streamline the hiring process and connect you with pre-screened candidates who match your criteria.

3. Effective Interviewing and Selection

Once you've attracted a pool of qualified candidates, it's time to conduct interviews. This is where the real work begins—interviews give you the opportunity to assess not only the candidate's skills and experience but also their fit within your company culture. In a small or growing business, cultural fit is just as important as technical expertise.

Create a structured interview process to ensure that you're asking the right questions and evaluating candidates consistently. Beyond asking about past experience and qualifications, dig into their problem-solving abilities, teamwork skills, and adaptability. Ask them to describe situations where they've had to overcome challenges, work under pressure, or collaborate with diverse teams. You want to understand how they approach real-world problems, not just theoretical ones.

It's also important to assess their passion for your business. Are they genuinely excited about your mission, or are they just looking for a job? A candidate who believes in your company's vision is more likely to stay engaged, work hard, and contribute meaningfully to your success.

In addition to traditional interviews, consider practical tests or assignments that simulate tasks they'll actually perform in the role. This will give you a more accurate sense of their capabilities and work style.

4. Onboarding and Training

After hiring the right people, the next critical step is ensuring they feel welcomed, prepared, and supported as they begin their new roles. Onboarding is often overlooked, but it's an essential process that lays the foundation for long-term success.

A well-structured onboarding process helps new hires get up to speed quickly, understand the company culture, and build strong relationships with their colleagues. Provide them with clear expectations, role-specific training, and access to the tools they need to succeed. Don't just throw them into the deep end—ensure that they have a mentor or manager to guide them through the first few months.

Training should also be an ongoing process. As your business evolves, so should the skills and knowledge of your team. Investing in professional development not only improves individual performance but also boosts morale and retention rates. Encourage employees to take on new challenges, attend industry events, and continuously learn and grow within their roles.

5. Fostering a Positive Team Culture

Once you've assembled your team, the next challenge is fostering a positive and collaborative culture. A motivated and cohesive team is essential for growth, and this is achieved by creating an environment where people feel valued, respected, and supported.

One key to building a great team is to encourage open communication. Promote transparency in all areas of the business and create a safe space where team members can share ideas, concerns, and feedback. Regular check-ins and team meetings allow for collaboration and ensure that everyone is aligned with the company's goals.

Recognize and celebrate team achievements, both big and small. Employee recognition goes a long way in boosting morale and showing your team that their hard work is appreciated. Whether it's through formal awards, shoutouts during team meetings, or small gestures like team lunches, showing appreciation fosters a sense of belonging and motivates employees to continue performing at their best.

6. Empowering Growth and Autonomy

As your business grows, you'll need to delegate tasks and responsibilities effectively. Empower your team by giving them the autonomy to make decisions and take ownership of their work. This not only boosts their confidence but also encourages innovation and creativity.

Give your team members the space to contribute their ideas and explore new ways of doing things. Encourage collaboration across different departments and allow people to take risks within their roles. When employees feel trusted and supported, they're more likely to go above and beyond to help the business succeed.

7. Retaining Top Talent

Building a team is one thing, but retaining top talent is another. Once you've found the right people, the goal is to keep them engaged, motivated, and loyal. Competitive compensation, benefits, and growth opportunities are important, but so is creating a workplace where people feel valued and connected to the company's mission.

Regular feedback, opportunities for career advancement, and a supportive work environment will keep your employees happy and reduce turnover. If your team feels like they're part of something bigger than just a paycheck, they'll be more likely to stay with your company long term.

Conclusion

Hiring and building a team is one of the most important—and rewarding—tasks you'll face as an entrepreneur. By hiring the right people, creating a positive and collaborative culture, and providing opportunities for growth, you can build a team that will help your business scale and thrive. Remember, your team is the backbone of your success, and investing in their development and well-being will pay off in dividends as your business grows.

Adopting a Mindset for Long-Term Success

As an entrepreneur, the path to success isn't always linear. There will be moments of triumph, but also plenty of challenges and setbacks. In these moments, what sets successful entrepreneurs apart from the rest is their mindset. Adopting a mindset for long-term success is crucial for navigating the unpredictable journey of building a business, staying motivated through tough times, and continuously growing.

But what does it mean to have a mindset for long-term success? It's not just about having a positive attitude or making quick decisions—it's about cultivating a deep-rooted belief in your potential, being open to learning, and remaining resilient when things don't go as planned. It's about staying focused on your end goal, even when the road gets rough, and making choices that align with your larger vision.

1. Embrace a Growth Mindset

One of the first steps in adopting a mindset for long-term success is embracing a growth mindset. A growth mindset is the belief that your abilities, intelligence, and skills can be developed through dedication, hard work, and learning. This contrasts with a fixed mindset, which assumes that talent and intelligence are static traits.

Entrepreneurs with a growth mindset see challenges and setbacks as opportunities for growth rather than as obstacles. They understand that failures are not final but rather stepping stones that lead to success. This mindset helps entrepreneurs stay focused on improvement and innovation, continuously evolving their skills and strategies as they build their businesses.

For example, instead of seeing a failed product launch as a sign of defeat, an entrepreneur with a growth mindset would view it as a learning experience, analyzing what went wrong and using that information to make improvements for the next attempt. This approach fosters resilience, adaptability, and a continuous desire to learn, which are all key components of long-term success.

2. Cultivate Patience and Persistence

Building a successful business doesn't happen overnight. There's no magic formula or shortcut to success. Achieving long-term goals requires patience, persistence, and the willingness to put in the work, day after day, even when progress seems slow.

Entrepreneurs often experience moments where it feels like they're working tirelessly without seeing the results they desire. During these times, it's easy to become disheartened and think about giving up. However, successful entrepreneurs understand that patience is an integral part of the process. They're willing to keep pushing forward, even when they can't immediately see the rewards.

The key is to stay focused on the bigger picture and remember that success is a marathon, not a sprint. Small, consistent steps over time can lead to substantial growth. It's essential to avoid the trap of impatience and to remain committed to your vision, understanding that each challenge you face is part of your growth journey.

3. Develop Emotional Intelligence

Emotional intelligence (EI) is the ability to recognize, understand, and manage your own emotions while also recognizing and influencing the emotions of others. As an entrepreneur, having high emotional intelligence is critical for building strong relationships, managing stress, and making sound decisions.

When you develop emotional intelligence, you're better equipped to handle the highs and lows of entrepreneurship. You become more self-aware, able to manage your emotions in tough situations and avoid reacting impulsively. This helps you maintain a sense of calm and composure when faced with difficult challenges.

Emotional intelligence also helps you connect with your team, partners, and customers on a deeper level. By understanding the emotions and motivations of others, you can communicate more effectively, build trust, and foster collaboration. These skills are essential when working in fast-paced environments or navigating conflicts.

As you cultivate your emotional intelligence, you'll find that you're able to manage both your own stress and the pressures that come from managing a business with greater ease. This emotional resilience is a powerful asset for long-term success.

4. Be Open to Change and Adaptability

In today's fast-changing business environment, adaptability is one of the most important traits you can develop. Technology, customer preferences, and market conditions are constantly shifting, and to stay ahead of the competition, you need to be flexible in your approach.

Successful entrepreneurs don't cling to outdated methods just because they worked in the past. Instead, they remain open to new ideas and are willing to pivot when necessary. Whether it's adopting new technology, adjusting your business model, or reevaluating your strategies based on new market insights, adaptability ensures that your business remains relevant and competitive.

Adopting an adaptable mindset means being willing to take risks, experiment with new approaches, and learn from failure. It's about seeing change not as a threat but as an opportunity for growth and innovation. By embracing change, you'll not only survive in the business world but thrive.

5. Prioritize Long-Term Vision Over Short-Term Gains

It's easy to get caught up in the allure of quick wins—seeking immediate gratification through short-term tactics or pushing for fast results. However, focusing solely on short-term gains can be detrimental to long-term success.

Successful entrepreneurs are always thinking ahead, aligning their actions with a broader vision for the future. They set long-term goals and make decisions that will position their business for sustainable growth, even if it means forgoing immediate rewards. They understand that true success takes time, and it's the slow, consistent effort that leads to meaningful outcomes.

This long-term focus helps you maintain a sense of purpose and direction. Even when faced with setbacks, you'll be able to stay motivated because you know that each step you take is bringing you closer to your ultimate goal. By prioritizing long-term success over short-term wins, you build a more resilient and sustainable business.

6. Build Strong Habits for Productivity and Focus

Success in business often comes down to the small daily habits that accumulate over time. Building strong habits for productivity and focus is essential for achieving long-term goals. Entrepreneurs who consistently show up, work efficiently, and maintain a high level of focus are more likely to stay on track and reach their objectives.

This could mean establishing a morning routine that sets you up for success, blocking out time for deep work, or creating systems that help you stay organized and on top of important tasks. It's about minimizing distractions, staying consistent, and taking care of both your mental and physical well-being.

Good habits also include taking regular breaks, practicing mindfulness, and making time for self-care. It's easy to get caught up in the hustle, but maintaining a healthy work-life balance is essential for staying energized and motivated over the long haul.

7. Foster a Sense of Purpose and Passion

Having a deep sense of purpose and passion for your business is the fuel that drives long-term success. When you're passionate about what you do, it's easier to stay committed during tough times and to push through challenges with resilience. A strong sense of purpose also helps you stay connected to your "why"—the reason you started your business in the first place.

Passion is contagious, and when you're passionate about your business, it inspires your team, customers, and partners. It creates a positive, motivated work environment and strengthens your company's culture. It also helps you differentiate yourself from competitors who may not have the same drive or enthusiasm.

Conclusion

Adopting a mindset for long-term success is about more than just ambition—it's about developing the mental and emotional tools needed to navigate the ups and downs of entrepreneurship. By embracing a growth mindset, staying patient and persistent, being adaptable, and fostering a sense of purpose, you'll position yourself for lasting success.

Remember, success doesn't happen overnight, and it's the mindset you cultivate today that will shape the future of your business. Stay committed to growth, keep learning, and trust that the work you're doing now will lead to long-term rewards.